LEAVING KAYSERI

A JOURNEY OF ONE HUNDRED YEARS

GREGORY KETABGIAN M.D.

2015

Avid Readers Publishing Group

Lakewood, California

The opinions expressed in this manuscript are those of the author and do not represent the thoughts or opinions of the publisher. The author warrants and represents that he has the legal right to publish or own all material in this book. If you find a discrepancy, contact the publisher at www.avidreaderspg.com.

Leaving Kayseri

All Rights Reserved

Copyright © 2015 Gregory Ketabgian M.D.

This book may not be transmitted, reproduced, or stored in part or in whole by any means without the express written consent of the publisher except for brief quotations in articles and reviews.

Avid Readers Publishing Group

http://www.avidreaderspg.com

ISBN-13: 978-1-61286-319-1

Printed in the United States

LEAVING KAYSERI

"The Armenians are afraid of forgetting the past; the Turks are scared of remembering it. Turkey cannot change the past, though it can face it."

Hasan Cemal (Grandson of Cemal Pasha)

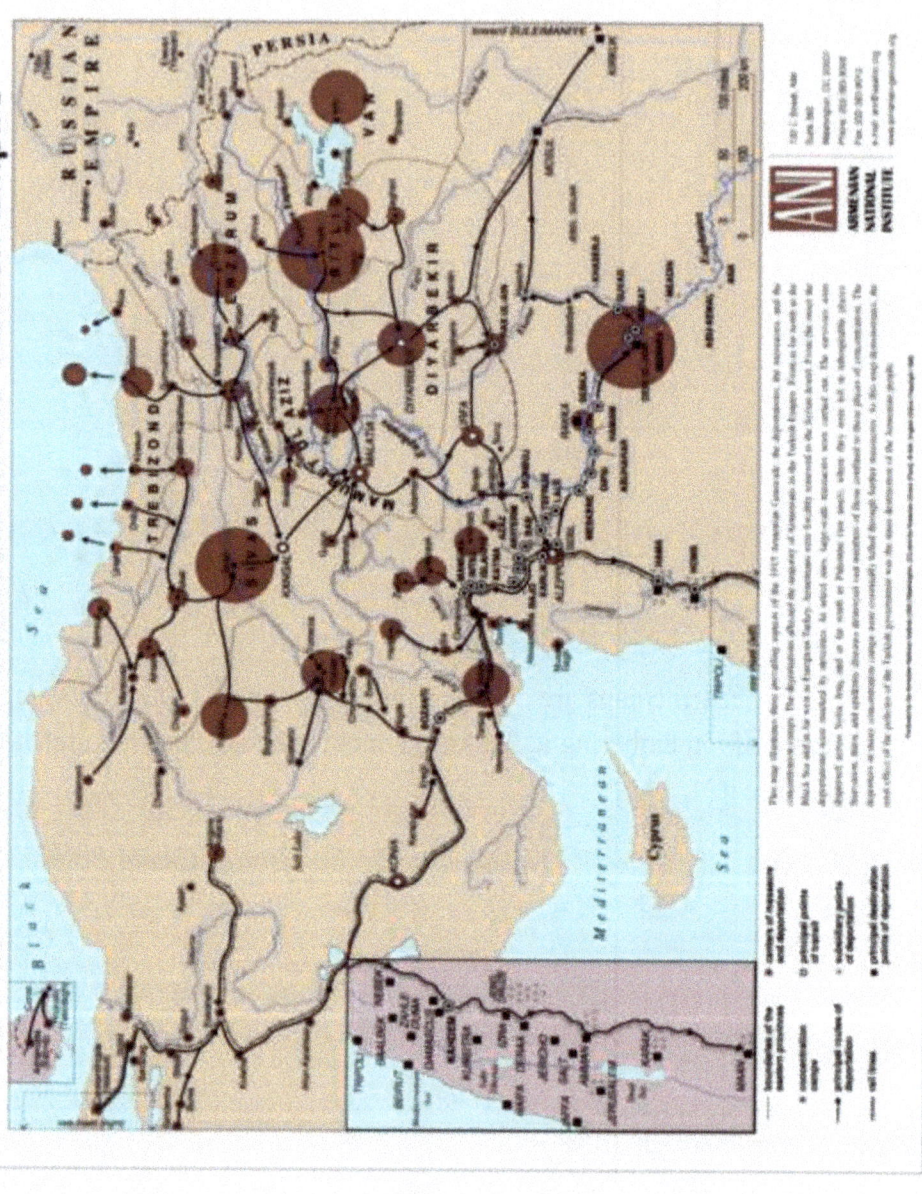

The 1915 Armenian Genocide in the Turkish Empire

CONTENTS

The Beginning 1
    To Memory (Poem) 5

Chapter 1
    Stories My Father Told Me 7
    War Prepartions and Talas 9
    Talas to Wawona House 12
    Jihad 16
    Looking for a Safe Haven 18
    Groong (Poem) 19
    Guns and Beatings 20
    Of Locusts 21
    Locusts (Poem) 22
    Among Those Hanged 23
    Prisons 25
    Political Parties 27
    Korzitch on the Kitabjian Roof 28
    Archbishop Balian's Role 29
    Arrest of Krikor Kitabjian 31

Chapter 2
    Deportation Orders 33
    A Good Fortune 34
    Looking for Our Homeland 34
    On a Deserted Distant Road (Poem) 35
    Ottoman Turkish 37
    St. Toros Church in Evereg 37
    Leaving Kayseri 40
    Bozanti on the Way to Adana 40
    Bozanti 40
    Corpse Covered Field 41
    Fields of Katma 48

Chapter 3
    The Road to Aleppo 49

To Ride a Bike	49
Sebil	53
The Funeral Procession	54
Bab and Victoria	54
Tetif	56
Aramig in Tetif	56
Tilling the Land (Poem)	57
Of Lice, Typhus and Death	59
Meskene to Abu Harrara	62
My Sister Hranoush in Abu Harara	63
The Arab in the Syrian Desert	63
Rakka	65
Taxicab Driver in Istanbul	66
Zeyarat	66
The Visitor (Poem)	69
Picnic at Abughalghal	72
Handful of Grass (Poem)	75

Chapter 4

On the Way to Deir el-Zor: Sebka	79
Merat Nahiye	81
Arous Ana	83
Merod	83
The Golden Tooth	84
Deir el-Zor Bridge	85
The Pocket Knife. (Poem)	86
Deir el-Zor Kurds	87
Working in Deir el-Zor	88
Near Death Experiences	89
A Role Model	90
Mardinsi Bedros	91
The British Are Coming	92
Turkish Propaganda against the Armenians	94

Chapter 5
Aleppo! 95
Making a Living 96
Raki, Basterma and Cats 98
Return to Gesaria 101
The Hidden Gold 101
Worthless Lead Bars 101
Killing Grandmother's Children 103
Traitors 103
Massacre of Returnees 104
Protestation to the Creator of This World. 105
They Come and Go (Poem) 110

Chapter 6
Meeting Mother 113
Marriage and Children 114
Broken Window 114
The Arab Landlord 119
My Maternal Aunt Vahidé 122
Bed Bugs and Aleppo Boils 125
The Old Arab Farmer (Poem) 127
The Village 128

Chapter 7
My Mother 131
Morning Chores 138
Rue Hamra, Beirut 139
Shiralarda 142
Convicted to Hard Labor 145
Beirut, Summer of 1945 145

Chapter 8
Ramadanieh Gas Station 149
The Store of Bustan Keleb 151
Barone Hotel 153
They Did Not Succeed 155
The Piano 156

Soot..158

Chapter 9
Coming to America..................................... 161
Leaving Beirut 161
Hamden High... 169
Poetry in Elementary School 170
Tzitzernag (Poem) 172
Skokie, Illinois... 173
Summer of 1955 and Jobs 176
Leaving Chicago on "Route 66"........................180

Chapter 10
Uncle Parsegh 183
Boredom and Mischief 184
Book of Poems on the March 185
"Nerkacht" Repatriation.............................. 187
Think Wisely 193
Civil War in Beirut, Lebanon..................... 195

Chapter 11
The Armenian Language 203
The Last Armenian (Poem).........................204
The Future 205
The Final Journey 206
Disappointments and Depression 206
Poem: The Days of My Life....................... 207
Unforgettable and Hellish Times 211
The Journey (Poem).................................... 212
Letter to My Father (Poem)........................213

Ending
Ending 215
The Old Oak Tree (Poem) 218

Appendices

Advice to My Nation.......................................219
Genealogy of the Kitabjian Family (Partial)............222

    Genealogy of the Matossian Family (Partial) 223
    Deed to home in Kayseri for Setrak Kitabjioglu ... 224
    Deed to home in Kayseri for Karkour Kitabjioglu ... 225
    Translation of deed by Taner Akcam 226
    Deed to home in Kayseri for Setrak Kitabjioglu ... 227
    Documents: Military ID Card Syrian Passport 228
    Ship Schedule 229
    Syrian ID and inside of passport............................... 230
    National Cultural Museum Publication 231
    Receipt from National Historical Museum (2)........ 232

Gesaratsi Stories 234

Glossary 239

Pictures and Maps Acknowledgments 245

Bibliography 247

Acknowledgments 249

LEAVING KAYSERI

The Beginning

This is my father's story. He and his family were uprooted from their native Kayseri in central Turkey during the beginning years of World War I by the Turkish government, controlled by the *Ittihad ve Terrakki* party members (Committee of Union and Progress, CUP). This is the history of the Kitabjian family during the Armenian Genocide of 1915. They suffered through deportation, robbery, famine, massacres and disease. Two members of my father's immediate family died during the march to Deir el-Zor in the Syrian Desert and were buried by the roadside. Altogether, ten members of the extended Kitabjian family perished.[1]

It is also a story of survival, having been subjected to all those indescribable atrocities that my father and his family endured against amazing odds. It is **a journey of one hundred years**; leaving Kayseri and continuing on endlessly through generations to disparate parts of the world looking for a "Homeland." As I have been searching in my memory to write these pages, it has become more obvious to me how much my father's experiences have affected us. It explains why he was so cautious in preparing us for the future and how this behavior of his impacted us.

It is also a story of the "Wandering Armenian." This was a group of people composed of survivors or orphans whose parents or family members were killed or died of disease and were wrenched away from their homeland to which they could **never**

---

[1] My grandfather Krikor had two brothers, Garabed and Setrak who were killed after being arrested in Kayseri in 1915. One of Setrak's children died during the deportation. Among his two sisters, Gulizar and her three children all perished, while her son Garabed Mooradian, who had immigrated to Boston before 1915, remained the only survivor of his family. The family of the other sister Hnazant Odabachian, some of whose members had previously moved to Aleppo survived except for one child who had died on the way.

return. It was the difficult task of trying to make it in a foreign country, after being subjected to the traumatic stresses of the Genocide. Having lost all their belongings, wealth and properties, they had to start from scratch, initially in Aleppo, Syria, a Muslim Arab country and later on in Lebanon, Soviet Armenia and Southern California. They were exposed to foreign languages, different cultures and mores, and a support system that was fragmented due to their being scattered around the world and being subjected to the process of assimilation that was already taking place.

These processes also affected my uncles and cousins. The family of one of my father's brothers, Uncle Haig suffered under the Communist regime after repatriating to Soviet Armenia. Additionally they endured numerous limitations following the Armenian independence of 1991 and the Karabagh conflict. The latter resulted in the blockage of the borders of The Republic of Armenia by Turkey, which has lasted over two decades.[2] The family of my father's middle brother, Uncle Parsegh experienced firsthand all the misery of the war in Lebanon and the subsequent difficulties in immigration and transition to the U.S. All of this again shows that the effect of the Genocide is ongoing, being experienced by the subsequent generations that have been cast here and there in the wide world, away from the safe haven of a homeland and the support base of their kin.

This is also our story. Initially growing up in a Muslim-Arab country; then coming to the United States, trying to adjust to the new surroundings and finding ourselves in a quandary in deciding which standards of mores, culture and language to adopt.

---

[2] Nagorno-Karabakh (Artsakh in Armenian) is a historic Armenian region that was under Azerbaijan's rule during the Soviet era that proclaimed its independence during the breakup of the Soviet Union. A six year battle ensued between the Armenians and the Azeri side and presently is in an unstable cease fire situation with most of the contested region under Armenian rule.

LEAVING KAYSERI

All of this was taking place while we were trying to compete and succeed in the fields we had chosen. Looking back at the whole experience, I realize that we felt great anxiety and stress which we were not aware of at the time but used it to energize us to go forward.

This is also an attempt to preserve our past history; since we belong to the last generation that still has some collective first hand memory of these episodes through contact with our parents and other Genocide survivors. It is an effort to collect and save some of the details of the events that will disappear when we are gone. I regret that we were too busy with our everyday lives earlier and did not take on this task until the previous generation was no longer here to be queried. Still, I hope that future generations will value the efforts made here.

My father, when asked to put his memories on paper, was reluctant to do so. He claimed that it was too painful and was afraid he would become further distraught and depressed. He said he would be reliving those terrible events all over again.[3] *Fortunately, he was willing to use an old Panasonic cassette tape recorder of mine to record his experiences until 1978.* These were translated into English by my sister, Shaké Balekjian and her husband Garbis and were edited and digitized by their son, Gary Balekjian. To preserve my father's memoirs as he expressed them on the tapes, I have used an *italic* font for his voice. They have been partitioned and titles added to allow the expression of our related experiences and to avoid monotony. No parts of his tapes were deleted or altered but some portions dealing with *Advice to*

---

[3] My father manifested some of the symptoms of Post-Traumatic Stress Disorder, although I believe it was controlled by sheer effort on his part and only manifested itself during episodes of high fever and other stressful situations.

My Nation can be found in the appendix. Explanatory notes were added where needed by the use of parenthesis and footnotes.

I have also included parts of the transcript of his interview in 1970 by a graduate student from UCLA, Garo Mardirossian, in the Armenian Studies Oral History Project under Dr. Richard Hovannisian's guidance. I have translated it from the Armenian on the CD provided to us. All highlighted sections in **bold** letters are mine but all segments in *italics* are my father's voice as preserved on the tapes.

There were also additional episodes and descriptions that my father had related to me and other family members through the years, which I have included as well as how these have affected us as children. The remaining essays deal with life in Aleppo as well as in Southern California and how we were affected by the whole experience. The free form poetry is mainly an emotional expression while the work was in progress.

Through the years, I have had occasion to come in contact with a fairly large number of Genocide survivors who immigrated to the United States. Listening to their stories and dealing with the effects of the trauma they had endured, increased my realization of the enormity of the crime. I believe that this unforgivable act against our nation has been etched on our DNA[4] and cannot be erased. To document this experience is mainly to honor the memory of the generations of Armenians lost during the Genocide and the generation of survivors that went before us. I do not think we can ever forgive or forget.

---

[4] Yehuda, Rachel and Bierer, LM, Transgenerational transmission of cortisol and PTSD, Progress of Brain Research, 2008; 167: 121-135.

LEAVING KAYSERI

To Memory

Running, after the rain, moisture hanging
On fresh leaves of spring
Through trails
Looking at streets past, to briefly peek into the past.
To revive old memories before
Forever they are lost.

We strive to look through the avenues
To relive the lives of our forefathers
But are they lost forever
In the crevasses of our cortex
Only to visit us early hours of the day
As if it has been etched on our DNA?

Let us run, relive, create anew.
Eager next generations are at the door.
Not to allow these memories to languish,
To pulverize like yellow acid paper in old books.
                              Gregory Ketabgian[5]

---

[5] Refers to jogging through Cape Cod neighborhood with my daughter Tamara, trying to identify streets from the past. Poem dedicated to Tamara.

CHAPTER 1

Stories My Father Told Me

"Quick! Wake up, your father insists on telling you about the massacres. He is running a high fever again." It was my mother who was waking me and my two sisters up on my father's persistence. He was susceptible to frequent sinus infections that would spread to his face and cheeks with a demarcated red swelling and high fever. During these febrile episodes, he would become delirious and would insist that we come to his bedside to listen to the atrocities he suffered during the Armenian Genocide. He with his family and most of the Armenian women and children of Kayseri were forced to march from the middle of Anatolia to Deir el-Zor in the Syrian Desert.

"The Kurds and Chechens are coming down the hills on horseback with their swords and guns pointed at us while we are marching. I can see it right in front of my eyes. They are robbing us of our possessions in and around our tents. They are ruthlessly slaughtering the defenseless people. They are cutting off the hands of women to get to their bracelets and rings, cutting off their heads or abducting and raping the younger women in spite of their screams. I can clearly hear it now in my ears."

"Meanwhile, the Turkish *gendarmes* (policemen) are doing nothing to protect us. Instead, after the Kurds are finished pillaging and killing the people, they are following them into the hills and discharging some rifle shots and then coming back to us claiming that they have protected us by driving the Kurds away and demanding two gold pieces from each family. Liars, thieves! *Vahshi Millet!* (Savage Nation)."

"I wanted you to know how we survived the massacres, and don't you forget it. Now you can go back to sleep, so you can be well-rested for school tomorrow. I want you to do well in school

CHAPTER 1

and succeed in life. This is not a permanent place for us to live. It is not a safe homeland for a Christian people to be living in a Muslim country. The butter that is churned in a Muslim *tulum* (animal skin) is never sweet."

His fever had come down after the medications that my mother had given him. We were living in Aleppo (Haleb), Syria during the end of World War II and Syrians had achieved independence and gotten rid of the vestiges of the French Mandate.[6] Having survived the massacres, my father and his family had reached Aleppo from Deir el-Zor in 1919. Meanwhile my mother's family had come from Antep (Gaziantep) to Aleppo in 1921 after the French forces had withdrawn south from Turkey to Syria, leaving the Armenian fighters in the Antep War without any support.

* * *

One day my father came home early from work having developed another sinus infection and wanted to start treatment with warm compresses to the face, while inhaling steam from a pot full of boiling water, with his head and neck covered with a towel.

"I went to the doctor today," he said, "and he again prescribed *solfato* (sulfa pills) and sinus irrigations. I told him that these have been useless in the past but he had nothing better to offer. But he said that they have just discovered a new cure for this infection in Europe which will cure it overnight, if given by injection. He said that the medication is in short supply and is only being used for the troops. It is called Penicillin and it comes from a mold."

After that my father would eat all the bread that had mold on it! Bread in Aleppo had no preservatives and would get moldy within

---

[6] The French Mandate was created after WWI to administer some of the regions of the Ottoman Empire that were outside the jurisdiction of the Turkish government.

one to two days. We used to get fresh bread daily from the baker around the corner from our house.

Of course, eating all the moldy bread in Aleppo did not cure my father's sinusitis until he received a series of Penicillin injections after the war had ended.

*   *   *

Fast forward to 1966: During my internal medicine residency at the Los Angeles County/USC Hospital, while on the medicine consultation service, I was called to see a lady on the ophthalmology ward who had developed a high fever with a red demarcated swelling of the left face and cheek post-operatively from an elective eye operation. When I saw the patient, right away it reminded me of my father's facial appearance. The resident next to me wanted to know what it was. "Erysipelas" I said. I showed a classic picture of it in Harrison's Textbook of Medicine. "And what is the treatment for it," he asked. I said "Penicillin."

The following section in italics is from the beginning portion of my father's tape recordings:

War Preparations and Talas:

I am the son of Krikor and Arousiag Kitabjian, Artin Kitabjian, Gesaratsi goldsmith. My dear children: In 1915 the Turks massacred one and a half million Armenians and we were among them. I am going to talk to you about it and I want you to listen to me.

In July of the year 1914, Germany and Turkey jointly declared a war against England, France and Russia. In

CHAPTER 1

and around Gesaria[7] *(Kayseri in present day Turkey) they were beating large drums, telling the people that war had been declared. The city of Gesaria was built on a plain. The city used to be hot, dry and dusty during the summer months.*

People owned orchards [in Talas], where they went during the months of July, August and September. It took one-and-half hours on horses or donkeys to reach their farms in the mountains.

There were four roads. One day the government instructed the police to block these four roads. They met the people who were coming from their farms, asking them to dismount. Then they seized their animals. The Turks took all the horses and the donkeys and gave everyone a receipt, saying that at the end of the war the government would return their animals. The people walked home.

Lots of people who heard about this hid their animals. This law applied only to the Armenians and Greeks. The people used to go to the city in the morning and return to their farms in the evening to have a good night's sleep.

After the Turks gathered everyone's animals, the Armenians went and rented animals from the Turks for the day so they could go back and forth. A few days passed this way. They put declarations on the walls saying that the government had gathered enough animals and that from then on, everyone could keep theirs.

---

[7] According to Ottoman census of 1914 out of a total population of 263,074 in Kayseri, 52,192 were Armenian. Of these 48,659 belonged to the Gregorian-Apostolic Mother Church; 2,018 were Armenian Protestants; and 1,515 were Armenian Catholics.

LEAVING KAYSERI

Family portrait of Krikor Kitabjian (my grandfather) in Kayseri in 1909. The photograph survived the deportations of 1915 since it was mailed earlier to a cousin, Parsegh Odabashian, living in Aleppo and later in Damascus, Syria. Standing from left to right: Arousiag Kitabjian, Hranush, and Krikor Kitabjian. In front seated from left: Artin Kitabjian (my father), his maternal grandmother, Perlantin Benlian, with Haig Kitabjian in her lap and Parsegh Kitabjian. (Photo by Photographkaniye Ergias, Kayseri. S. Mostichian, G. Timourian, 1907. (The date written in a different colored ink pen in the back of the picture is in error since Haig Kitabjian was born in 1908 and looks like one year old in the picture.)

CHAPTER 1

One Sunday morning, while my father was at church, I took our donkey to the bazaar. "We have a good donkey here." The clowns who saw it liked it. I sold it for four Ottoman Turkish gold pieces. I took two gold pieces, and the rest was to be paid to my father later in the week. My father went to the bazaar every morning. One day he saw that they were bargaining on our donkey. They sold it for four and a half Ottoman Turkish gold pieces. They told my father, "Here are your two gold pieces." He thanked them and came to the store.

A few weeks later they started picking up all the other animals, these liars. Therefore, we left our farm and came to the city. All the foreign schools, the Armenian, the British, the French and Greek schools were closed; therefore I was going to the store with my father every day.

Talas to Wawona House

...To my life's experiences in Los Angeles:
"I planted this tree as a cross to our dead."
Zaven Surmelian.

The house in the Eagle Rock-Glassell Park section of Los Angeles at 4129 Wawona Street, bought in 1958, was situated on a triangular lot with a small frontage. It extended downhill into a large backyard from where the house was positioned.

The following spring, when bare-root fruit trees became available for planting, my father wanted to plant a number of them in the back yard. He wanted to reproduce the orchards that the family owned in Talas near Kayseri. Talas was a summer resort, being at a higher altitude on the foothills of the Erciyes (Argaeus) Mountain. It was much cooler there than it was in the city. My father used to tell us that he and his uncle used to go further up the mountain to the ice fields during the summer months, cut big chunks of the ice,[8] pack it in hay and bring it to Talas and put it in the basement to cool the lemonade. A similar experience is portrayed by Elia Kazan in his autobiographical book and film "America, America" in which his father and uncle are portrayed growing up in Kayseri.[9] His full name was Elias Kazancioglu.

My father had told us that he had spent the best times of his boyhood in Talas, where life was relaxed. He spent time in the wilderness and had a small caliber shotgun with which he learned to hunt birds. The last summer before the Genocide, the military had confiscated all the weapons from their homes.

* * *

We bought two of each kind of fruit tree including peach, plum, apricot, nectarine, quince and pomegranate. My father also got cuttings of fig from my maternal uncle Sarkis's yard. Near the end he had close to fifty fruit trees, since he had also planted additional apricot trees that he had cultivated from choice seeds.

As the trees grew and gave ample fruit, he would pick, arrange them in a flat cardboard box, and place it in the refrigerator. Then he would call us to come and get them before they spoiled. They were the most flavorful fruits one tasted since they had ripened on the trees. Later, as the apricot trees multiplied from the choice seeds, he planted one in each of his children's backyards.

He fought a constant battle with birds and ants, mainly on the apricot and fig trees. He put together a contraption to scare the

---

[8] Kazan, Elia. "*America, America*". Popular Library, 1964

[9] Kazan, Elia. "The Arrangement". Stein and Day, 1967. P. 429-430. In this book Elia Kazan relates finding a picture of Mt. Ercyes (Argaeus) near Kayseri hanging on the wall in his father's bedroom in New York after his father had passed away, indicating that his father, who was born and grew up in Kayseri, had never gotten the old country out of his mind and had wanted to be taken back there when he was terminally ill.

CHAPTER 1

birds away from the trees. He attached a barbecue rotisserie motor to a pole, hanging pie plates from it. When the birds came to the fruit, he would turn on the switch to rotate the contraption to scare the birds away. Unfortunately after a few weeks, the birds got used to his innovation and went under the trees and still picked at the fruit.

Mount Ercyes (Argaeus) during summer. (Elevation 12,848ft.)

* * *

The lower story, as well as the backyard of the house on Wawona Street were unfinished. My father and I completed the downstairs bedroom, sitting room and the bathroom. It became my bedroom and study during the last two years of college and later during medical school and postgraduate training. We poured concrete for the patio and for a fountain. It became the center of family activities during summer picnics and barbecues.

The laundry area was already completed. There was also a gas oven where my father cooked *lahmajoun* (Armenian pizza) with the help of my mother who would have already prepared the dough along with the meat and vegetable mixture earlier in the morning. Most of the time my maternal aunts Arous and Rahel as well as my sisters, Shaké and Arpiné, would come to help. Mother usually prepared the dough and others would put the mixture on top and hand it to my father who would be sitting in front of the oven, perspiring from the heat but making sure that both the top and bottom of the *lahmajoun* were cooked just right. He had fixed special paddles for the dough to be placed on and be transferred into the oven. The whole process was set up to function like an assembly line. They usually cooked enough to be able to distribute to five families, plus some to be consumed on the day of production. Most of the working members of the family would be alerted the day before to "*lahmajoun* day" and no one would miss the luncheon on that day. The *lahmajoun* tasted best hot just out of the oven.

* * *

My father remembered that a distant cousin of his from Talas, James Kitabjian, had come to California after the massacres of 1909 and had escaped the Genocide. Through a Gesaratsi friend at a church picnic, he found out the address of his store and had me drive him there to meet him. Valley Cleaners was in Alhambra on Valley Boulevard. We went in to meet his cousin, who did not seem too excited about the prospect of meeting us and we did not have too much in common, besides preliminary conversation. We left the place quite discouraged. My father had always maintained that people who emigrated to the U.S. eventually lost interest in their family connections, as if they had been "vaccinated" against it. He also thought that "maybe the cousin was afraid we might ask for some monetary assistance."

While in medical practice in Pasadena, a pharmaceutical detailer said that he played handball at the YMCA with a Johnny Kitabjian, a fireman in the Pasadena Fire Department. Later I met Johnny, who happened to be one of the sons of the cousin from Talas. He was a very warm, appreciative and God fearing person.

CHAPTER 1

His children were all active in the teaching profession and church ministry and were highly regarded by all who knew them.

* * *

Continuing with my father's tape recordings, here he is describing declaration of Jihad by Cemal Pasha:

Jihad

> *One afternoon we saw that the market was full of police officers. The government proclaimed that all the people, whether they were Christian or Muslim, should gather at the big square in front of the government building. A high official named Cemal Pasha[10] had come from Constantinople to clarify the people's minds.*
>
> *The square was filled with all sorts of people. They blew a horn. Everyone got quiet. This famous person, Cemal Pasha, came out of the room where everyone was clapping and he started to talk. "We are declaring a Jihad[11] today against England, France and Russia. These Christian governments want to eliminate our religion, occupy our lands, all we own from the face of the earth. We want our kingdom and our people to shed our last drop of blood [to defend our country]. Everyone, the clergy with his staff, the shepherd with his crook, is everybody ready to do his duty? Do you promise?" All the people shouted, "We are ready!"*

---

[10] Cemal Pasha (Ahmed Cemal, Cemal pronounced Jemal) was the third member of the chief perpetrators of the Armenian Genocide, the others being Mehmet Talaat, the mastermind, and Ismail Enver.

[11] This is the only reference found of Jihad being proclaimed by Cemal Pasha in Kayseri. A holy war was declared against the Allies and Christians minorities (by Sheikh-ul-Islam) on Nov. 14, 1914 with the full knowledge of the Germans. Rubin, B. & Schwanitz, W. *Nazis, Islamists and the Making of Modern Middle East*, Yale Univ. Press, 2014.

LEAVING KAYSERI

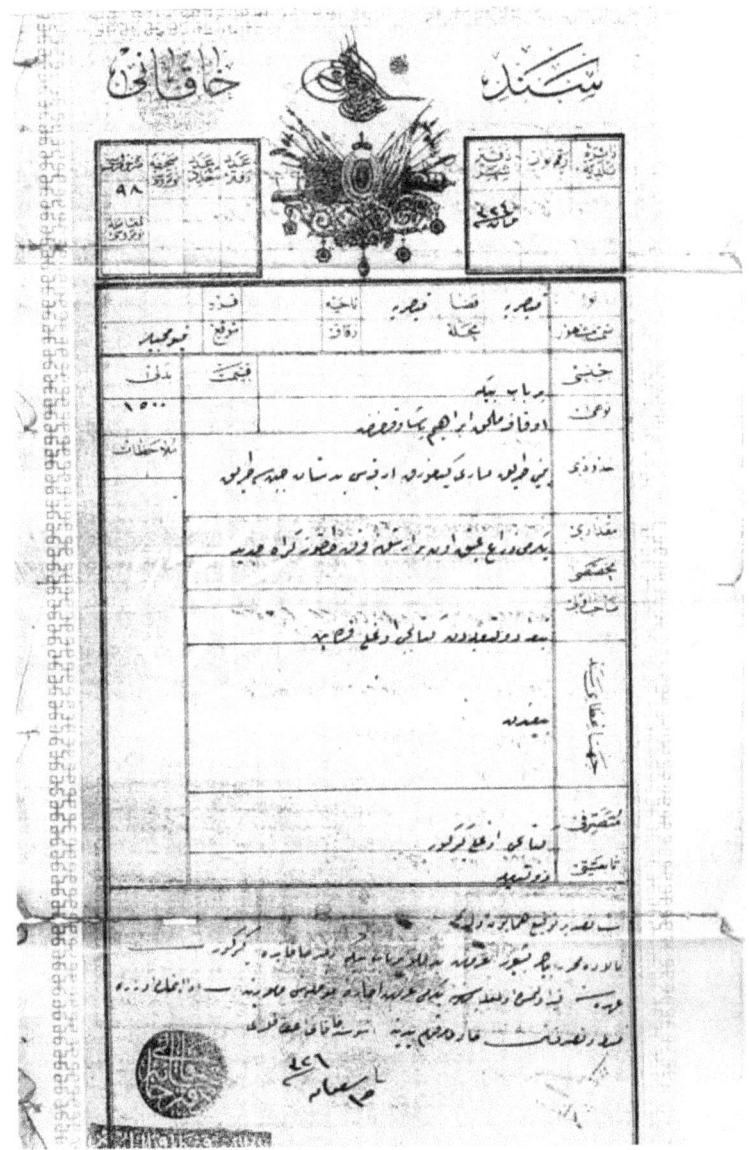

This is the copy of the deed to the house in Kayseri. This one was for Kitabjioghlu Kerkor. These were found with the genealogy papers of my aunt Knarig Kitabjian in the possession of Araxy Kitabjian in N. Andover, MA. There were also 2 similar documents named for Terak Kitabjioglu, most likely referring to great-uncle Setrak. Copies of the two additional documents and translation of one of the documents by Taner Akcam are found in the appendix.

CHAPTER 1

All the Christians' faces turned to stone. The people went straight back to their homes.

A few weeks later the Turks started to collect everything that was needed or not needed to fight the war. They took everything from the Christians' stores and filled up large warehouses and they gave everyone a small receipt for whatever goods they had taken. The people had not seen anything like this before. We were watching with great anxiety.

Looking for a Safe Haven

In spite of the escalating violence against them, most of the Armenians remained in their towns and villages of Anatolia before the Genocide. They felt that this land was their homeland and they thought that the government would protect them against danger, especially after the new constitution of 1908, which promised the minorities additional rights. However, there were increasing episodes of violence culminating in the Adana Massacre of 1909, where thirty thousand Armenians were killed and their homes and businesses looted and burned. It became more and more obvious that life in those lands would not continue to be peaceful.

Apparently, the father of the James Kitabjian of Talas, was killed during a conflagration there in 1909, that being the reason for his and his mother's migration to America before 1915, thus avoiding the Genocide. [12]

Those with the means and education tried to emigrate to Europe and America. Others had left to make a living with the intent of returning back to Turkey after making some money. Still others were in self-exile due to political activities or due to having run

---

[12] The Adana Massacre in 1909 was the first **Holocaust** of the 20th century. The populace that had taken refuge in the churches was incinerated after the churches were set on fire.

into conflicts with the local Turks or Kurds and would leave the country for a while instead of depending on the nonexistent justice to defend the Armenians. *Bantoughtutune* (Exile or Sojourner-worker) and love of the homeland and family has had an amazing influence in creating its own literature, poems and songs. Songs like *Groong* (Crane) and *Tzitzernak* (Swallow, see Chapter 9) are two examples of this genre.

Groong (Crane)
(My translation)

Groong, where do you come from, I am a slave to your voice,
Groong, don't you have news from our country,
Do not rush; soon you will join your brood,
Groong, don't you have news from our country?

Gomidas Vartabed[13]

My Grandfather Krikor and his two brothers took a trip to canvas the regions around the Mediterranean Sea, to see where they should emigrate. They visited Cyprus, Egypt and Jerusalem and the decision was made to emigrate to Egypt. But after their return to Kayseri, the political situation seemed stable and the older brother Garabed decided that they should stay put since they were making a good living and felt safe there. This was one year before the beginning of the Genocide. Unfortunately, both he and his brother Setrak were arrested, taken to jail and tortured. Later they were taken towards Tomarza and killed alongside other Armenian men. Garabed was stoned to death.

---

[13] Gomidas Vartabed was a cleric who traveled throughout the villages and towns of Armenia and wrote down and thus saved a large number of Armenian folk songs in use by the people in late 19th and 20th centuries. Words and music source: "*Tankaran Haygagan Erkeru*" (Treasury of Armenian Songs). Badmakrian, A. and Missirlian, E. Pub. Vosgedar Printing, 1940s, Cairo, Egypt. p. 82.

CHAPTER 1

Next two sections from my father's tapes show further deterioration of life in Kayseri leading to the Genocide:

<u>Guns and Beatings</u>:

  A few weeks later, a new government proclamation was pasted to the walls of the city. We ran to read this proclamation that was about guns. They had decided that whatever guns, revolvers, shotguns and everything else that did not belong in a kitchen, like large knives, including all swords and sabers were to be returned and brought to a room next to the government building. At the door, there were two gendarmes. Inside, there were secretaries seated on all four corners who wrote your name, your last name and your address. They gave you a receipt and said, "We're going to search your houses and if we find any other types of guns, you will be jailed and the gallows is the punishment."

  The registration went on for a few weeks; in addition, they were beating the people. They knocked on your door at night. They called your name. You came out. They said: "Come with us." They took you to city hall, and on the way they told you that the government had questions to ask you. Next, they took you to a large prison. Some other person came and called your name and took you to another room. The chief said, "Look, you have another big gun; why didn't you give that to us? Are you trying to fool us? Lay him down immediately." He ordered to the soldiers and said, "Give him twenty or thirty hits at the soles of his feet." "Effendi (Sir), I don't have it." Again twenty or thirty more hits with a stick. The man fainted. They pushed him aside and they poured a bucket of water on him.

  The man woke up in the middle of the night. The gendarmes saw that his feet were bleeding; he was swollen all over, all black because they had whipped him up hard.

They told him, "Go home, rest and we'll call you again. At that time you can bring your Martin (rifle) with you. Otherwise, you know what will happen. Didn't you see it? There are different types [of guns]."[14]

I can say that out of one hundred males, seventy or eighty were often beaten this way. This lasted for one month. Men would not venture outside their homes. They were scared and they couldn't come out anyway because their feet hurt. You would guess that the city was crying.

Of Locusts:

That year there was a big pestilence of locust, the likes of which I had never seen before. In the cold of the night they were inactive but once the sun came out, they would warm up and start flying. It looked like there was a big dark cloud in front of the sun.

The night before, the government instructed the neighborhood guards that we would be collecting the locusts. The guards would wake up everybody at two or three at night. With bag in hand, we would go outside. Each person would have to fill his bag with five kilos of locust before the locust would start flying again. Then we had to wait in line so that we could deliver the bags. We would line up and enter the city via the road they chose. After that, everyone returned to their homes.

---

[14] The beatings were conducted to incriminate additional names and to obtain material for the court-martials to follow. Vahakn Dadrian, "The Agency of "Triggering Mechanisms" as a Factor in the Organization of the Genocide Against the Armenians of Kayseri District." *Genocide Studies and Prevention* 1, 2 (September 2006): 107-126.

CHAPTER 1

Locusts

Harbingers of famine
Coming in swarms
Dark clouds
Blocking out the sun.

Five kilos in the bag
Before daybreak
Passing by city center;
Gallows!

Forerunner of times
Not seen biblical,
Watching in disbelief
Omen of catastrophe.

Locusts,
Harbingers of calamity.

Gregory Ketabgian, 2011

The locusts had covered the entire city. But they purposely would take us to the Turkish side beyond the city hall, so their vegetables would not be damaged. This way they could grow and sell the vegetables back to us.

When they were bringing the people back, [on June 15, 1915] *they had us pass right in front of the city hall gate and what a sight we saw! There were twelve people who were hanged. They were the leading Armenians in Gesaria. Their names were written on their chests. They were the intellectuals, the priest, the teacher, and the wealthy, all well-known people. When we saw this, our spirits broke.* [15]

Among Those Hanged

The following section and similar ones that follow are from the taped interview done by a graduate student from UCLA Oral History Project.
GM=Garo Mardirossian, AK=Artin Kitabjian:

GM: Were both parties present in your city?
AK: Both parties were there. But the *Hunchakian* party[16] worker [Minas Minasian] gave the government the list of the names, the money and the whereabouts of the guns. After extensive amount of beating he had given up. But, the *Dashnak*[17] party head,

---

[15] Names of the first eleven hanged on June 15 were;
1. Garabed Jamdjian, copper merchant, neutral. Active in the community. Pointed out as a Hunchak.
2. Karnik Kouyumdjian, active for self-defense, involved in accumulation of guns. Neutral.
3. Avedis Zambakjian, Neutral merchant, with Kouyumdjian, involved in procuring guns.
4. Kevork Vishabian, an exemplary Dashnak.
5. Garabed Tcheydamian, a Hunchak.
6. Yacoub Siudjian, a Hunchak.
7. Chalghige Mirigan, Hunchak. A bomb was found in his house.
8. Hagop Khayerlian, a gunsmith. Dashnak. Guns were found in the walls of his house, but was arrested instead of his brother who hid in the mountains.
9. Hagop Merdinian, had become neutral on his mother's insistence, Bombs from another's residence were transferred. The gallows' rope broke twice and a wire was used for his third hanging.
10, Hagop Aslanian, was a young coppersmith who built the bomb casings as part of his job.
11, Minas Minasian, a Hunchak, teacher, and a traitor who was hanged with his victims. (12). Haji Hovannes Nevshehirian was hanged on June 16, a goldsmith.
From Alboyajian, Arshag A. *The History of Armenian Gesaria*. Cairo, Egypt: Hagop Papazian Press, 1937 (in Armenian) pp. 1412-1416. Kevorkian, Raymond, *The Armenian Genocide. A Complete History,* I.B.Taurus, London, New York, 2011p. 517.

(Note: there are discrepancies of some of the names between these two sources.)

[16] Hunchakian (Social Democratic Hunchakian Party, members called "Hunchak") was founded in 1887 to liberate Armenians from Ottoman rule.

[17] Dashnaktsutyun (Armenian Revolutionary Federation , ARF, members called "Dashnak") founded in 1890 as an Armenian left wing party to fight against Ottoman injustices.

CHAPTER 1

Kevork Vishabian, I knew them all, said he was the only one and he was hanged.

GM: Did he not give the names of the members?

AK: No. Neither the names nor where the guns were hidden. They kept him for a few days. They told him that if you do not give us the information, you will be hanged. Whether he talked or he did not, he was hanged.

GM: The *Hunchakian* who divulged the information, did they hang him?

AK: They hanged him as well. He was one of the twelve that was hanged.

GM: He was in the twelve that was hanged.

AK: Do you want the names of the ones hanged? I know a few of them. Der Aristakes Demirjian, a priest, he was a well-known priest and used to give good sermons.

GM: What was the reason why they hanged the priest?

AK: They had questioned him, blaming him to be a revolutionary. They blamed him for possession of guns. They hanged him. This was at the beginning, in 1915. It was to discourage the population so that they would not rebel against the government. They had already collected all the guns.

GM: Who else was among the ones hanged?

AK: Among them there was Garabed Jamjian[18] a very famous, rich person, who also had a position in the government. They found a Martin rifle in his home.

GM: Is Martin a type of gun?

AK: Martin is a big rifle.

GM: Not a Mauser?

AK: No, it is called a Martin. You put in 2-3 bullets and it fires them one after another.

---

[18] Garabed Jamjian was paraded after his arrest through the Muslim section of the city while in chains with the rifle they found in his home as the "Armenian King" to demonstrate the power the Ittihadists had over the rich Armenians who had extensive government connections. From Yapoujian, Hagazoun, *"Rumdigin Memoirs"* Dbaran Atlas, Beyrout, 1967. (in Armenian) p188-189.

LEAVING KAYSERI

GM: Did they hang him because they found a gun in his house?
AK: They hanged him also for being very rich. There is also Ohannes Eff. Boyajian. He was the principal of my school. He was also hanged...
GM: Is it still in front of your eyes?
AK: They had hanged them at night, but we were returning from collecting the locust early in the morning; they made us pass in front of them. They were there hanging. We passed in front of them. We went crazy. We were young people. All the fathers were taken away already; do you understand? We were 14, 15, 16 year old boys; we had gone to collect the locust. We saw all that and we went home. What misery we experienced after that!

My father's description of the deteriorating situation continues:

Prisons:

> *After this, every morning, three or four people would be hanged.[19] We lived this way for a few weeks. We were thinking of things that we had never thought about. It so happened that all the city hall's jails and a number of additional rooms were filled with prisoners.*
>
> *Now they started thinking about different methods. People who were in prison for ten to fifteen years; they let them go free. All of these were Muslims. They were murderers. Under the government's authority, they formed groups of these prisoners and chose rugged valleys outside the cities and sent them to these locations.*
>
> *A few days later the Armenian prisoners, of which there were many, were taken away in caravans of carts to be*

---

[19] By the end a total of 55 men were sentenced to death by hanging. Dadrian, Agency, p. 110.

CHAPTER 1

massacred.[20] Everyday eighty or one hundred men left under the guise that they were being sent to Aleppo. They said they wanted to empty the prisons, but then on the other hand, they were picking up more people here and there, the forgotten ones. They tried to say that since Gesaria was in the war zone, they wanted to remove us so that no harm would come to us. We had no evidence of this. They always talked this way.

From all these groups who had left, only two arrived safely in Aleppo and they were robbed and penniless. One caravan had eighty-seven people and the other caravan had hundred twenty. We were still in Gesaria.

Picture taken of the first Armenian prisoners in front of the Kayseri jail in early spring of 1915. The picture was provided by Steve Kurkjian who has done extensive investigation into the identity of the individuals and their fate. Photographer was Gulbenk (Chichekian)[21].

---

[20] A secret group was set up by the perpetrators of the Genocide (Special Organization; *Teskilat-I Mahsusa*) composed mainly of criminals and irregulars for slaughtering the men in gorges and canyons under the direction of Dr. Bahaeddin Sakir, a physician.

[21] Steve Kurkjian, NAASR lecture; "Kiss My Children's Eyes," personal communication. Sept. 2006. and *Armenian Weekly*, April 22, 2014.

Political Parties

GM: Did you join any revolutionary activities?

AK: My father had a friend in the revolutionary party. He had approached him to enroll him as a member. My father had told him: "I do not understand what you mean by revolution. Since you tell me that you need money, let me give you some money, but do not write my name in your book," because they used to be afraid of the government that something written could get discovered.

Later it became obvious. This was in 1894-95 when my father was still single. Forty three people were arrested from Gesaria, three of which were revolutionary *Hunchakian* members. They took them to Ankara, which was our *vilayet* (regional center)…….. Well, my father was within that group of 43 men. They were tied together in groups of five and sent in carriages to Ankara. If one had to go to the toilet, all five of them had to go with him. Then all five of them had to come back together to enter in the carriage. Forty of them were questioned and not one of them knew or admitted to know about the revolutionary activities. Do you understand? The other three admitted that they formed these groups to defend themselves. They sent the forty back to Gesaria; the other three were hanged in Ankara. The forty were told that if their names came up in other lists, that they would be hanged also. My father says that it was Easter Sunday when they got back home.

GM: Was your father in that group?

AK: Yes, since he gave money, the man wrote his name down.

GM: He had written his name down since he gave the money and the officials considered him a revolutionary.

AK: Forty of them had answered like my father, "We do not know anything," that they only donated money, they had no other interests.

GM: Was this during Sultan Hamid's time?

AK: Yes, During Sultan Hamid's time.

GM: Did you help at all during 1915?

AK: No, I did not get involved at all. My father told me that he did not want his name written but the man had done it. My father had told me, "Never join any revolutionary parties." And I never joined any parties. But no one asked me either. Since I was only 17, and in those days you were still considered a child.

"Korzitch" on the Kitabjian Roof

In 1909 while in Gesaria, my father remembered an incident that had taken place on the roof of the house of one of their relatives. A *Hunchakian* Party *"korzitch"* (party worker)[22] was demonstrating against the Ottoman government and trying to get the people in the neighborhood agitated to join him in a demonstration. This was a man with long hair and with a leather bag hanging from his shoulder. The gendarmes arrived and the officials called the military to come to surround that area of the town where Armenians were living. The rebel put his hand on his bag and threatened that if anyone came close, he would throw a hand grenade at them. Both local Armenians and the Turkish officials had a meeting to avert the disaster; otherwise it would have meant the massacre of the Armenian population. It was agreed to give the person safe passage out of Gesaria that night to avoid bloodshed. This type of poorly planned demonstrations by political parties demanding Armenian rights and independence gave the Turkish government ample excuse to attack the general population and got the native Turks and Kurds enraged. These events would usually culminate in pogroms involving pillage, killings, rape and the abduction of women and the burning of homes and stores.

---

[22] Azad Vostanig (Melkon Mirsaksian) called Satchli (Hairy) by the Turks, was on top of the Hunchakian library, above the Kitabjian building in Baghche-Bashi section. Alboyajian, Arshag, pp.627-628.

LEAVING KAYSERI

Archbishop Balian's Role

GM: Did you hear or see any revolutionary activity in your region before 1915?

AK: Yes. In 1908, minorities were promised more rights. In 1909, the Adana Massacre took place. On the same day that it took place, they were also going to massacre the Armenians in Gesaria. Two to three days prior, a *Hunchakian* party member had come to Gesaria... He had rented a room from our relatives, the Kitabjians, and was living there. In the afternoon of the Adana massacre, a group of soldiers came and surrounded that building... Our Archbishop, Dirtad Balian, a very brave priest, was called by the government and was told that if this person does not leave by that night, the whole population would be massacred. Do you understand? After hearing that, the priest returned to arrange for the person's transfer to save the city and they sent him out.

GM: Without shooting him?

AK: Yes. Two other persons from the revolutionaries left the city with him in a carriage. I do not know in which direction they went.

GM: The people with him, were they *Dashnak* or *Hunchak*?

AK: Both parties were represented.

* * *

The other incident involving my father that convinced him that political parties were functioning irresponsibly and not thinking about the general welfare of the Armenian people, took place later in Aleppo in 1920. He and a good friend of his had attended a *Dashnak* Party meeting in an attempt to help the nation's poor and destitute population. During the first meeting of the new members, their superior informed them that he was going to spin a revolver and when it stopped, whoever it was pointing to, had the duty of assassinating a well-known Armenian person in the opposing party. The revolver stopped pointing at my father's friend. When

CHAPTER 1

the superior would not hear any excuses, he took the assigned revolver reluctantly. A week later the body of my father's friend was discovered in an area just outside of town, having committed suicide using the same gun.

Sometimes members from a radical party would come to my father's store in Aleppo and ask him which party he belonged to. This used to irritate him since he knew what their response would be when he answered. He would say that he was not a member of any party and he was *chezok* (non-partisan). Then they would say that if you are not with us, that means you are against us. However, he was a lifetime member of AGBU (Armenian General Benevolent Union) and supported them, since he considered them to be nonpolitical and nonsectarian.

* * *

My contact with the functioning of Armenian political parties, although not as dramatic, came after I had arrived in Chicago. It was 1956 and we were having Sunday dinner at my brother in law, Popkin's parents' home. His father was a self-educated man who kept up with national news and literature. He once had a friend over for Sunday dinner who was a *Dashnak* party member. This person started to question me about my background. Following the negative experiences my father had with political party activists, he had instructed us to remain neutral and not to join any parties. This gentleman started telling me and the group about the murder of Archbishop Ghevont Touryan in New York. This event had followed a confrontation regarding the presentation of the Armenian tricolor flag at the 1933 Chicago Century of Progress International Exposition where the Archbishop was to speak. The Archbishop was murdered later in New York, as he was getting ready to celebrate mass.

Although a number of men from the *Dashnak* party were convicted and served jail sentences, the guest claimed that

Archbishop Touryan was actually killed by the opposing party. However the *Dashnaks* who were in church that Sunday were blamed. I thought that his position seemed counter to regular common sense, since the Archbishop was supporting the opposing party's views and its supporters would be unlikely to kill him. Everyone, including Popkin's father, all of a sudden stopped eating and after a short period of silence, they agreed that what I said made sense. Subsequently, I started receiving a gift subscription to the Armenian Review periodical from an anonymous benefactor.[23]

<u>Arrest of Krikor Kitabjian</u>: My father's description of his father's arrest:

> *One night the doorbell rang; we opened the door and a policeman was asking for my father. He said he should put on his coat and accompany him. On the arrest warrant of the police officer, it was written "Krikor Kebabjian." In the old Ottoman characters, which used the Arabic alphabet, if you put a dot at the bottom of the letter it became "kebab," if you put it on top it became "ketab." Regardless of the fact that it said "kebab" instead of "ketab," they still took my father.*
>
> *There was a big fountain near our house where a group of men had been asked to wait. The police had gathered them from the neighborhood to take them to the palace jail. On the way to the jail, my father came to an understanding with one of the police officers by promising him two Turkish gold coins. The policeman agreed because of the confusion regarding the spelling of his name. My father came back home with the officer and we gave him the gold pieces. For the following three hours we were very happy. The minute the sun came up, there was another*

---

[23] Phillips, Terry, "*Murder at the Altar*". Hye Books, Bakersfield, CA 2008. p. 16-26.

CHAPTER 1

knock on our door. When my mother opened the door, it was the police officer who said, "We want Krikor to come out; it's not a mistake. That is your name." And they took my father away. Could he say anything about the money given previously?

* * *

Sometime later I got a telegram from my father who had landed in Aleppo, saying, "Send me twenty Osmanian (Ottoman) gold pieces immediately." His address there was Krikor Kitabjian, Victoria Hotel, Khandak Street. We got the news that he had received the money.

"In a few weeks we are going to Hama," my father wrote. In March 1915, my father was exiled to Hama.

Gesaria was in silence. There were still men in hiding; they were afraid of being noticed, therefore they did not want to risk being seen outside. Only the women would dare to go outside for household needs.

Mihran Yazujian, a traitor, a dog to his people, did many bad and treacherous deeds. He betrayed numerous people.[24]

Later, one day in the afternoon, we learned that an Armenian man by the name of Sebastasi Mourad[25] was hanged in the front gate of city hall. He was a partisan. The government did it on purpose to break the will of the remaining people. All communication with the outside world was broken. We did not know what was happening around us at all.

---

[24] Mihran Yazujian, also called "Pidj (Bastard) Mihran," a Dashnag traitor, was the main identifier in Gesaria. Eyewitness accounts of him; "Sitting in Jafer-beg jail, legs crossed, a cigar in his mouth, with a dog's smile, would identify the newcomers and whether he would decide to save them or convict them for torture by the beast, commissar Besim." From Alboyajian, pp.1411.

[25] Murad (Hampartsum Boyajian) a Hunchak leader and a parliamentarian was transferred from Ayash jail, having been arrested on April 24, 1915 with the other intellectuals from Constantinople. The hangings were carried out at a local area called *Komurluk* (Coal Pit). Dadrian, Agency, p.117.

Chapter 2

Deportation Orders: My father's description of how the deportations started:

> *A few weeks passed. On August 10, 1915, the government issued a proclamation which was glued on the wall near the corner of the large fountain by our house. I saw that a lot of people came out to read it and I ran to read it too. It was written: "By the order of the King, for the next three months, these places that are in the war zone will be evacuated. The caravans will be traveling in the direction towards Aleppo."[26]*
>
> *The names of the streets to be deported were written in front of each evacuation date. The first caravan was to leave on August 15, 1915; the second caravan consisting of people living on the next three streets were to leave on the 16th. Our and my uncle's street names were written next to the date of August 17th.[27] This is when we realized the pain in our hearts. During the five remaining days, they let us sell our household goods to the Turks so that we would have some pocket money with us. We accepted whatever price they gave us, because we were going to leave and didn't know when we were going to return.*

---

[26] "Being in the war zone" was a common official excuse for the deportations and is still used by deniers of the Genocide. This logic does not fit with the location of Kayseri in central Turkey, because it was far from both the eastern front with Russia and the western front with the European Allies.

[27] The five Armenian sections were; Bahje-bache, Dicharechar, Icharychar, Jawikyou Malacy, and Kechy Kapou. He does not state which section their house was in, but says that they were close to Beouk Chesme (Big Fountain). Most likely it was Bahje-Bache where the other Kitabjians also lived. It was named after a triangular plot of land that was used to grow vegetables during the summer months (Personal communication; Steve Zurnacian).
The Kitabjian's goldsmith store was in Vezir Khan Section.

CHAPTER 2

There is a saying in Turkish, "Ana Baba Gunu", meaning "chaos." It actually amounted to a form of looting.

A Good Fortune:

We were going to leave the city on August 17, 1915. Two days earlier, on August 15th, a police officer brought a piece of paper and added, "You are not going to leave." When we asked the reason why, he said, "You are going to stay because dentist Mgrdich Demirjian requested us to keep you here since you are the goldsmith he uses to fix the gold crowns." I went to see Mgrdich Effendi and he said, "I am going to stay and I want you to stay as well." When I asked him how he felt about treating Turks as patients, he said, "Whatever happens to me, the same will happen to you; let's just get through these bad days."[28]

After I returned home, we thought about it. We had already hired the animals that we were going to take with us. We were in a dilemma. This was such a good fortune which we didn't appreciate at the time. We realized it later.

Looking for Our Homeland

After nine plus decades following the Genocide, our culture and psyche has been so influenced by the enormity of the crime; the dispersion of the total Armenian population throughout the world has made members of our generation still feel like we do not belong to any specific land or feel attached to any location. Instead, we have substituted all of this with the quest for material goods and comfortable living situations in different countries

---

[28] It was later reported that dentist Mgrdich Demirjian had accepted Islamization for continued stay in Gesaria. Alboyajian. p. 1528.

throughout the world. In the true sense, we are actually people without a country.

My wife Alice and I took a trip to Eastern Turkey during the summer of 2006, a Pilgrimage to Historic Western Armenia, to see with our own eyes and to walk the grounds with our own feet the places that our fathers and forefathers had lived in and walked on. We felt haunted by the words of Avedik Isahakian[29] in the following poem (my translation):

On A Deserted Distant Road

On a deserted distant road
My caravan moves on peacefully.
Halt! Caravan. It seems to me that
My Motherland is calling me.

But it is all quiet around me
There are no sounds in this sun beaten desert.
My Motherland is indifferent to me,
My tender love is in someone else's embrace.

Proceed, Caravan. Take me towards
Deserted foreign lands.
And when tired, I will put my head down
Among hard stones, on top of thorns.

* * *

The old Armenian section of Gesaria was mainly in ruins. The walls of the houses made of dark volcanic basalt looked almost black and weather-beaten. A fairly wide, new boulevard had been forged through a portion of it. The homes on one side of the street were partially demolished; the remainders of the buildings were left exposed as if a tornado had passed over them. Could this have been another effort by the local Turkish

---

[29] Avedik Isahakian, lyric poet, writer and activist. (1875-1957)

CHAPTER 2

government to depict the previous Armenian population in a lower light, inferior to the Turks, to be debased, despised, dehumanized and hated?

Walking through some of the old streets, we came upon a fountain that still was functional, except someone had attached a garden hose and directed the water towards one of the houses that still had residents in it. Could this have been the fountain close to my father's home where the police led my grandfather Krikor, before they took him to jail prior to his exile?

People who were living there seemed like they were homeless settlers or nomads. Their children, when they saw us, started running after us begging, "Hello, Dollar." They also started throwing rocks when we entered the church courtyard that had tall walls and a locked steel door. The Soorp Krikor Lusavorich Church (St. Gregory the Illuminator) is still functional, having services twice a year. It has an Armenian caretaker who lives there with his family and is supported by the Patriarchate in Istanbul. The church was renovated in 1999 with the funds donated by two benefactors from Istanbul, but their names were purposely omitted from the plaque, because they feared additional taxation by the government.

Unfortunately, the Gumushian school building attached to the church did not enjoy such support and only the walls were remaining. There is no significant number of Armenian residents living in the surrounding area to support a school. This is the school that my father had attended before going to the Jesuit school for two years to learn French. Knowing some French had helped him during our residence in Aleppo, Syria because it was under the French Mandate and official business was conducted in French.

Ottoman Turkish using the Arabic alphabet and many Turkish words having Arabic roots, he was able to pick up the language fairly easily after arriving in Aleppo.

Ottoman Turkish

AK: I can also write in Turkish.

GM: With Arabic letters?

AK: Yes, with Arabic letters.

GM: The old Ottoman language?

AK: Yes, old Ottoman language, I read it well. If a telegram came to a neighbor I always used to read it for them. Actually, on the road to Deir el-Zor, there were deportees from Izmir [Smyrna at the time] with us. Do you understand? They wanted to request money from Izmir by telegram; they had exhausted their money. I wrote their telegram in Turkish in 1915. Turkey changed to the new alphabet after Mustafa Kemal came to power.

GM: After 1921-23.

AK: Yes, it was after 1923.

St. Toros Church in Evereg

We also visited the Armenian section of Evereg, now named Develi, which is on the southern side of the Erciyas Mountain. We came across a 200 year old hexagonal church that had been converted into a mosque in 1978. We were not able to enter the church since the door was locked; however we noticed that the Armenian character "E" signifying God within the "Sourp Erortutiun" (Holy Trinity) triangle above the entry had been chiseled out.[30] We also walked around the neighborhood and noticed some Armenian names on the doors. The most shocking experience for us was the street name on the telephone pole. It was, "Talaat Pasha Sokagi" (Talaat Pasha Street). We were sure that was not by sheer coincidence.

---

[30] During building restoration in 1998 it was discovered that fresco paintings of Virgin Mary that had been covered with whitewash in 1978 had once again become visible. Worship in the mosque was suspended until a decision was made to restore the paintings but to cover it with opaque glass so it would not be visible to the Muslim worshippers.

CHAPTER 2

Large fountain in Kayseri.

The side view of Sourp Krikor Lusavorich Church (St. Gregory the Illuminator) in Kayseri built mainly with dark basaltic stones.

The main altar of St. Gregory the Illuminator Church in Kayseri.

The deportation map representing the route, direction and the camps.

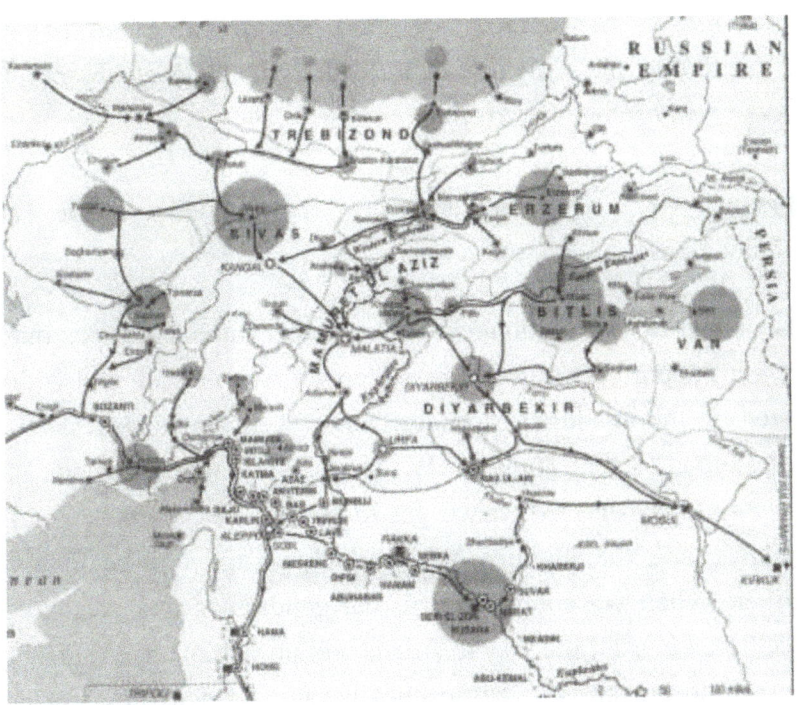

CHAPTER 2

Leaving Kaayseri: Father starting on the deportation route:

With my mother, four brothers and a sister, we left Gesaria on the third caravan on the evening of August 17, 1915. Rather than living a life of imprisonment in the city, now we were walking freely on the road, but we were still under the command of the one gendarme. In these few months, we encountered beatings, hangings and death. In addition, we had left all our possessions behind and were deported out of the city. We wanted to leave because we thought that it was better to leave rather than experience having your heart broken into pieces every day.

We left Gesaria. We had rented seven donkeys to help us reach Adana. We took the deportation path and started walking. The hardships and the misery were indescribable.

Bozanti On The Way to Adana:

When we arrived at Bozanti, the people who were leading the donkeys that had been paid for in advance deserted us. We had to rent oxcarts to reach Adana. The roads to get to Adana were all uphill and difficult to travel. There were many steep hills to climb.

Bozanti: Here, my father describes what happened at the Taurus mountain pass:

AK: I had rented 7 donkeys; I tried to rent a carriage, but the previous deportees from the six streets on August 15th and 16th had rented all the available carriages. There were no carriages left; we were forced to rent donkeys. We rented the donkeys to take us all the way to Adana. When we got to Bozanti, the caretakers of the donkeys took the supplies off the donkeys and refused to go any further. When we complained to the gendarmes that we had paid them to take us all the way to Adana and now they were refusing, he said, "I do not know. They cannot go any further; they were only supposed to go to Bozanti; having promised Adana was a mistake." At this point, they took the donkeys and left. There, we rented oxcarts and we went to Adana in them. We stayed in Adana for one day. From Adana to Osmaniye, they made us take the train so we could get there faster.

We stayed one to one and a half months in Katma. Then we continued on our way.

* * *

The following is an essay by an eyewitness deportee from Gesaria in the caravan leaving on August 16, 1915, preceding my father's departure by one day. Because there were a number of similarities in the direction travelled up to Katma (a large camp for deportees), I thought it might be helpful to have a translated portion presented here. The author's description of his experiences is in great detail and pictorially well presented. **It also highlights the reason why the animal caretakers unloaded their possessions at Bozanti.**

Corpse Covered Field:
A Chapter from the Turkish Monstrosities of 1915

Written by Arshavir Kaghtsrouni (Tatlian)[31] Translated from the Armenian by Gregory Ketabgian.

"My son, Yavrous, do not get down from the carriage; you can get caught, and get us into trouble," my poor grandmother was pleading with me. While sitting in the front of the carriage, she was guarding five of us children in a "wagon" similar to the American ones of the 1880s covered with a thick cotton material. Meanwhile I was again trying to slip out from the back of the carriage.

It was a hot and stifling August night. We had left the little towns of the Cilician plains about ten days ago, going towards Osmaniye, a center established for driven out *sevkiat* (deportees). Passed that town towards Syria, Arabia and Mesopotemia, everything was unknown.

---

[31] Arshavir Kaghtsrouni, "*Corpse Covered Field,*" *Artsakang*, p. 120-127.

CHAPTER 2

Among the deportees a few of those who were able to escape, both from their appearance and their stories, had caused fear and terror for us. Armenians from all locations driven out as "mouhajeers" (refugees) and sent to the killing fields were in a large and dreary tent city; even its being temporary was considered a misfortune. No one wanted to cross over the hill that darkened the northern horizon. According to the circulating rumors, all kinds of evil deeds were reserved for the Armenians on the other side of the hill. The escapee eyewitnesses were talking about the attacks by Turkish hordes, the massacre of caravans by armed *chetes* (band of brigands), the rape of young girls in front of their parents, the infants being carried off until they were distributed among the Turks and finally, the adults, men or women in groups being massacred in the valleys. Names of places were mentioned among which the most horror laden was a hell named Katma.

Our family was composed of my queenly-appearing and capable grandmother, my intelligent, lithe and courageous mother, my two brothers and my three sisters. My older brother was fifteen, but fortunately not large-framed. We were one of those taken out of Gesaria with the "second caravan" with the other 150 families (*August 16th*).

We had started on the road from Gesaria under the protection of a neighbor across the street. Three members of this good and caring family were Garabed Agha Ohanian, his gentle-hearted wife Nirze and their beautiful and angelic daughter, Zabel. The elder Garabed Agha Ohanian had undertaken the responsibility of fatherly protection for our family, there being no adult male with us. This patriarchal gentle man would not allow our rented four donkeys to separate from his three donkeys. And his partner, a good Turk, was accompanying him on a horse, to give them protection and the shadow of his protective arm was also benefitting us.

LEAVING KAYSERI

* * *

We reached the Bozanti pass which was the killing fields of Armenians from Gesaria and the surrounding areas in three days. At this point all of the keepers of horses, donkeys and carriages slipped away at midnight, like mercury and disappeared with their animals. This was in spite of their being paid to go all the way to Tarsus.

According to the latest information, they had gone and joined the Turkish *chetes* at the base of the mountains. The following morning they had attacked the unlucky people in the tents, robbed them of their valuables, raped the young girls including the children and killed with swords those who could not flee or hide. They had also destroyed all the tents and everything else that they could not carry with them. Thieves, murderous monsters!

Our family was saved by a mere difference of two hours from the first planned massacre for the Armenians of Gesaria on their journey to Golgotha, covered with thorny thistle and painted with Armenian blood. Two hours before that sinister dawn after the donkey caretakers left us, the monsters were sharpening their hellish appetites, their beastly teeth and deadly swords for the rape and bloody feast on the members of our group. Aware of what was to happen, our old and benevolent protector on horseback, not knowing where from, had obtained two oxcarts. After loading them quickly, we had gotten on the road slightly before daybreak. And the following day, by mixing with another "fortunate" *muhadjeer* (refugee) group, after traveling for a month we had reached Osmaniye migrants' road, passing through Tarsus and Adana. There, due to the turn of events, we became deprived of both our gentle neighbor's fatherly care and of the good Turk's protection.

By leaving this one month's narration of "travel odyssey" for another time, let me say this much that the "gifts" and bribes to win the good favors of each carriage driver and policeman at every new station, our monetary resources had reached to their lowest

CHAPTER 2

level. Due to the lack of funds compounded by the lack of protection and care, our condition had reached a desperate state. And our only remaining hope was our uncle, Djivan; and we knew where he was. Without him, like many other deportees, we had come close to our end.

Due to fortunate circumstances, this uncle, instead of being taken to the gallows similar to hundreds of Armenian men, was sent to Aleppo together with four captive friends. He was a uniquely gentle and honorable person gifted with superior qualities. He was well known as an expert rug maker. He was also one of those rare individuals able to interpret the Armenian notations, rare expert of eastern music, string instruments and especially a good player of the *oud* (lute). Because of these talents, the governor of Aleppo at that time had given him a certificate to be able to remain there, meanwhile his four friends were sent to Rakka, another arena for the killing of Armenians, where they were slaughtered.

The monster Talaat, the interior minister of Turkey, had demoted the governor of Aleppo on the accusation of being an Armenophile and had him exiled to one of the interior regions that had been "cleansed." But before that, my uncle was able to get the seal of the governor on his *vesica* (license) to be able to bring us to Aleppo without harm. He was also able to obtain a police officer named Mustafa *Chavoush* (Sargent) with an accompanying soldier who was going to Adana on official business.

Meanwhile, we had considered the copy of the telegram from the governor of Aleppo to our uncle to be a shield against *sevkiat* (deportation), but in spite of that, due to the uncertainty we were living miserable and difficult days, which felt like centuries.

Suddenly they came, Chavoush Mustafa and his friend soldier, and between them this life giving, angelic face of our "most capable" uncle. Since that day, the northern hill signifying death changed its fearful and terrifying appearance for us.

Armed with the license that arrived and with my Uncle's

resources, we were able to hire a larger than average horse carriage.

Following that, with the accompaniment of the two Turkish uniformed horsemen, we got on the road to Aleppo without fear. Then going through scary passages, cutting across barren lands always with the fear of death and being eyewitness to traces of unbelievable methods of sacrifice of the Armenian people, we reached the camp, which had been one of the most monstrous of all; even terrorizing from afar, its name was Katma. Here, although we were very close to Aleppo, we found the passage to be blocked.

Exactly around this time, the new governor of Aleppo had arrived and established himself there. It was none other than Zeki, the previous *kaymakam* (governor) of Gesaria-Evereg. Although he spoke Armenian, he hated and killed Armenians. A civilized outward appearance shielded him, but deep down he was a most beastly *Ittihad* monster. He had received the Pasha title and the governorship of Aleppo from Sultan Muhammed Rashid as recognition for his "heroic" efforts for the annihilation of Armenians. He had ordered the closure of the road to Aleppo. My uncle, having lost his previous secure position, was now in hiding.

When we arrived in Katma on that hot night, *Chavoush* Mustafa, aware of the changes, had advised us to get the work done with the local governor by "buttering his palm" and he, my mother and my oldest brother had gone to see the *kaymakam*, having given us strict orders that none of us get out of the carriage. This was the order that I was trying to defy, being curious about the things I had heard about Katma. My grandmother kept repeating; "Yavroum (my child), don't get out, you will be caught." But I had already jumped down, and after checking that no one had seen me, I quickly slid through the twilight and reached the other side of the crossroads. In front of me appeared a short, steep downhill area at the bottom of which along its length was a deep pathway. Further away was a wide field with uneven elevations with a row of small hills. Among the numerous stars, some were obvious and others were barely noticeable. Like a thin white veil transparent in some spots, clouds had covered the face of the moon. The light of the moon, similar to the nonexistent tears of the souls at a funeral, was filling the surroundings with gloom. In deadly silence, a group of Armenian deportees' tents were noticeable half buried below the distant eastern horizon. Towards sunset, at the side of the highest hill, a dark and deep cavity was wrapped in darkness.

My heart was already filling up with fear and grief when a threatening voice behind me shouted, "*Oulan, geavour pidgy*" (Hey, infidel's bastard). Terrorized, I remained nailed to the ground for a second. I had been noticed. The person to whom this voice belonged had to be a savage Turk. I was going to be caught and my grandmother's fears would be realized. I turned back and saw that it was an unfamiliar policeman, who fortunately was walking towards me very slowly. I was in the snare of peril. The only escape was towards the field. Desperate, after a moment's hesitation, I jumped down the hill as if fired from a bow into the pit where I fell after stepping on a soft matter. There was no time to either stop or think. Quickly I got up, threw myself into the field and started running towards the dark cavity. During my run, repeatedly I bumped against soft substances, fell down and got up a few times. At last I reached a half buried rock in the darkness of the valley where I could hide and for the first time I was able to take a deep breath and could turn back to look. The policeman was standing at the edge of the road but strange, he was not coming down to chase me. I felt a little safer and the terror of fear was replaced by thinking. What were those soft materials under foot?

The surrounding was covered with a terrible smell. I wondered! I wondered! I turned back towards the dark ditch. What awe, what a dimly presented horrible scenery. Human legs and arms pointed towards the air in irregular lines. Heads with appearance as if still alive scattered here and there, piled on top of each other. The black field that was covered with the corpses of my compatriots was transformed into a horrible and hellish cemetery of the suffocated and unburied children of my people.

It is beyond human ability to imagine the state of mind of a thirteen year old, although mischievous and active but still inexperienced, exposed to this unimaginable hellish scenery. But it is beyond reason and unreliable to try to explain his emotional state. It felt like a dagger's thrust deep into my heart. And having awakened to depression and to hopelessness, I had become stiff like a mummy. What beastly monsters, what cruel and evil humans!

Distant, indistinct sounds like echoes aroused me from vengeful thoughts. One was my mother's voice; "Son, where are you?" She was crying. The others were my older brother Yervant's and my sister Zabel's voices, who with emotional accent were yelling, "Arshavir, Arshavir Aga" giving my name. I pointed my gaze towards where the carriage was and on the edge of the road I noticed human silhouettes. They were walking, they were moving, and they were alive! My mother, brother, sister, Chavoush Mustafa and his soldier friend. The other unknown policeman was not around. I think I tried to shout, and having gotten energized, started walking half hurried and half cautiously towards the moving human figures.

I had come fairly close to the edge of the field. Being extremely careful and thinking it a piece of a rock, I stepped with my full weight on a protuberant earth. What horrendous surprise. The earth opened up under my feet and I got buried up to my knees and fell down on my face. During my fall, my left hand went a few inches into the dirt and I felt the lines and softness of a human face. I had stepped and fallen on the swollen belly of a corpse that had died not long ago and only covered with dirt, the thickness of a blanket. What permanent fear and dreadful feeling! I don't know how I did it, but with superhuman force I threw myself to one side.

CHAPTER 2

And then I felt the place I was lying on was moving similar to the previous nights, trak, trak, trak; the sound of the wheels of the carriage came to my ear, mixed with the sad sob, repeated hearty sighs of my bright grandmother's cry, "*Yavroum* (My child) didn't I tell you not to get out ?"

***Fields of Katma*:** My father describing their stay there:

> *The following day, they put us on a train intended for cattle and took us to Osmaniye. We started walking again, this time through Islahiye.*
>
> *We arrived at Katma. What should we see? All the fields of Katma were filled with people. They were all Armenian deportees. It was like a madhouse. We stayed there a few months. My mother was very sick. We lived under tents. We saw that there was a lot of illness there. The majority of the people had dysentery.*
>
> *During this time, we got news from my father in Hama that we should join him there. One day the town crier was calling, "Gesaratsi Artin Kitabjian, go to the train station. The train master wants to see you." What happiness! I went running. I entered the director's room, and I told him, "I am Kitabjian Artin." He said, "Look, my brother is the sergeant in Hama, he sent me a telegraph and telling me your father is there, and don't wait." After a minute I asked him, "Isn't it possible for us to go there on the train, Effendi?" And he said, "My lamb, the train belongs to the military." That's all.*
>
> *The following day, I sent a telegram to Hama that it is impossible for us to go there, "Father, if you can, you come here, instead."*

Chapter 3

The Road to Aleppo: Father resumes the journey:

> *We started going towards Aleppo, but we didn't succeed.[32] We got ready and hired a horse drawn carriage to take us to Aleppo. After Aleppo there were so many roads and deserts that awaited us. My uncles' families, Garabed and Setrak were with us; they had hired donkeys. My uncle Setrak's daughter, Victoria was having problems riding the donkey; therefore we convinced my aunt that she should travel with us. We wanted her to ride with us in our carriage. Her mother agreed to let us have the little girl. We reached Sebil* (public fountain) *near Aleppo.*

To Ride a Bike

My maternal cousin Hrair Dekmejian's father had a heavy British-made bike which he used to go to work at a delicatessen at the railroad station in the outskirts of Aleppo. As kids, we all wanted to learn to ride his bike, but our legs were too short to reach its pedals.

One Sunday afternoon, all three of us cousins were at Sebil where there was a tree shaded garden around an artificial pond which had an outdoor restaurant. It was a pleasant location for families to gather on weekends to relax and have *mezza* and kebab dinner.

---

[32] This edict preventing the Armenian deportees from entering the city of Aleppo was put in place by Salih Zeki Bey, who was the previous ruthless governor of the Evereg-Kayseri Sanjak, who was transferred to Aleppo and eventually to Deir-el-Zor by July 16 to replace the more lenient governors towards the Armenian deportees (Ali Suad Bey of Deir el-Zor). He was apparently fluent in Armenian. Near the end of the war he had amassed an amazing wealth and Talaat wanted him to return it to the treasury which he refused. Vahakn Dadrian (personal communication) and Kevorkian, Raymond, *The Armenian Genocide. A Complete History*, I.B.Taurus, London, New York, 2011. P. 663-664. Sarkissian Khacher, *Memories of Seventy Years*, G. Donikian, Beirut, Lebanon. (Armenian) p.438-440.

CHAPTER 3

We used to go there on Sundays with the families of my aunts and uncles. The cousins would have fun playing games and sometimes would get into mischief. I remember once cousin Hrair had brought a home-built toy, a sailboat and insisted on trying to sail it on the artificial pond. The sailboat floated to the center of the pond and sank. Hrair, in his effort to rescue the boat, slipped on the algae at the bottom of the pond and fell in.

This created a great deal of excitement amongst his mother and aunts, although there was no danger that he would drown, since the pond was only about two feet deep in the center. Hrair was extricated easily, but got reprimanded and had to have his clothes dried out in the sun.

The waiter at the outdoor restaurant would shout out the orders to the cook. My father would order the *mezza*, but would stress that the hammos be without olive oil, since the custom there was to drown out the hammos plate in two centimeters of olive oil. All the other customers would turn around and look at us when they heard that we ordered *"hammos bella zeit."* (Hummus without olive oil).

Sebil, as the name in Turkish signifies, was a public park with a natural fountain where Armenian deportees going to Deir el-Zor camped to rest periodically during the Armenian Genocide. Such camps were set up where there was a source of water for the pack animals, the horses of the carriages and for the gendarmes. The Turks would not allow the deportees to enter Aleppo.

This was my father's favorite location to take his out of town guests later when we were living in Aleppo, especially after they had enlarged the park with additional trees and fountains. I wondered if this location had additional significance for him, as he remembered his experiences during the deportation, especially the loss of his sister and baby brother. He would take numerous pictures of us, the children that represented the next generation.

LEAVING KAYSERI

Sebil Gardens in Aleppo with family members with a good view of the German and later French military fort up the hill. The picture was taken by my father with his Zeiss Ikon camera circa 1948.

There was a military fort up on the high hill on the east side of the Sebil gardens, which is seen in many of the pictures. The fort was probably built during the Turkish occupation of Syria. It was used earlier by German forces and later by the French Mandatory forces after World War I. The water source of the fort came from the valley. Apparently, my Cousin Zaven Khachaturian's father worked on maintaining the pumping system for this water supply during the French occupation of Syria after WWI.

The garden had a good-sized parking lot where we could practice riding the bike. Hrair had figured out a way of riding the huge bike by standing on the left pedal with his left foot while he put his right leg through the bars on the right pedal. He had to hold onto the handle bars while maintaining the bike tilted to the right to keep his balance. He was practicing it in the parking lot until he came too close to a black Ford parked in the hot Aleppo sun. He fell on the car and was pinned against it with the weight of the heavy bike. He felt like he was getting fried, until we pulled him and his bike off the hot car.

* * *

CHAPTER 3

I had a scarier experience trying to learn to ride the bike after I had gotten slightly taller. While practicing on the road to the Armenian Cemetery, which was downhill, I could not control the speed of the bike and headed straight towards a barbed wire fence. Fortunately, the bike got the brunt of the impact, and I got a number of cuts and bruises on my legs. When I got home, my mother noticed my cuts that were bleeding. I told her that I fell off the bike while riding on the back seat.

As I got older, I used to rent a bike from the bike rental guy in front of our apartment to ride to the Sebil Gardens on certain Sunday mornings, mainly for exercise. On one occasion, I ran into a group of older Armenian bikers and followed them on the road past the gardens. On the way back, a group of Arabs had blocked

Four cousins at Sebil Gardens in the summer of 1945. From the left: Mary Dekmejian, Zaven Khachaturian, Hrair Dekmejian and Gregory Ketabgian.

Sebil Gardens with the famous bicycle held by Cousin Hrair Dekmejian and with my sister Shaké seated. Front row from the left; Cousins Mary Dekmejian, Zaven Khachaturian, Gregory Ketabgian. Back row; from the left, Hrant Dekmejian, Vahide Dekmejian, my mother Beatrice Kitabjian, and standing Rahel Khachaturian.

the road ahead and were waving at us to stop. It was decided by the group leaders to ride fast to pass them up. The older boys were better riders than I was. I could not pick up enough speed to pass the Arabs and they caught me. They would not release me until the other bikers came back to meet their demands. The bikers stopped ahead and decided to come back to help me. It turned out that the Arabs wanted a tire pump that one of their members needed to pump his bicycle tires. I was released unharmed.

Sebil: Father's experience at Sebil during the journey:

When we arrived at Sebil, what did we see? There were hundreds of carriages waiting, which were kept out of the city; they put our carriage behind the hundreds of the other carriages and told us to follow them. There were a few gendarmes and there was one gendarme who was riding a horse. I approached this gendarme. I told him, "We want to go to Hama; we will pay you whatever you want." This man was holding a whip in his hand and with it he hit me

CHAPTER 3

hard in the neck and I thought that my head was cut off. I started crying.

The Funeral Procession

It was the custom in Aleppo to have a funeral procession to honor the deceased. The people attending the church services would later follow on foot the horse drawn carriage carrying the coffin all the way to the cemetery. The Armenian cemetery was some distance from the Karasoon Mangantz Church (Forty Brave Martyrs). At the time, it was outside the city borders. The procession passed in front of our house on Suleymanieh Street. Most people and vehicles would honor the procession and would not interfere with it.

During a funeral procession in 1953, my father and I, following behind a group of mourners were walking down a narrow street in Aleppo. There came a muscular Arab riding on a mule with a row of four other loaded mules following him, trying to force his way through the procession. We were towards the back of the group. I tried not to allow him to pass us, in spite of his shouts and curses. Next thing I know, I felt this amazing burning-tearing pain in the middle of my back. He had hit me with his whip. I touched the area, but could not detect any blood on my hand. At that moment, my father pulled me aside. He said, *"Khent es, Dgha?* (Are you crazy, son?) Let him pass." Later he said, "Don't you know that the law is on his side; we are a Christian minority in this country and have no rights. Don't ever risk your life to make a statement for an impractical cause."

<u>Bab and Victoria:</u> In the next 3 sections my father is describing sad events on the march:

LEAVING KAYSERI

I thought about my uncle's little daughter who was with us. Her family was on donkeys. They were slower, therefore they lagged behind.

The caravan started moving. I asked, "Where are we going?" They said, "Town of Bab." They drove us to Bab[33]. The man who was driving our carriage was Armenian, and his name was Aram. I said. "Aram, just hit the front wheel to a rock to break it. Whatever the price is, I'll pay double the amount so we can stop on the side of the road and they can catch up with us." I told him I wanted to stay there for the night, because I wanted to give the little girl back to her mother so that they would not be separated for the remainder of the trip. We hit the rocks quite a few times, but we didn't succeed. Therefore we had to continue on.

When it got dark, we rested a little bit. All of a sudden, we heard gunfire. The gendarmes who were with us had started firing towards the mountains. After a while, they came back. They said that whoever was shooting at the caravan had escaped; but that we were going to remain there for the night. In the morning when we woke up, there was lots of talk in the caravan that the gendarmes had spent too many bullets at night to save us. It was a nice ploy because they wanted two pieces of gold for each carriage. It was dark, therefore we couldn't see. The two gendarmes had gone by the mountains and actually they were the ones who were shooting.

We drove the carriage and arrived alive and safe in the village of Bab. The following day I gave the carriage driver two pieces of gold. I wrote a note and gave it to him so that he would take Victoria to the Diocese in Aleppo.

---

[33] Sarkissian, K. The villager's homes in Bab were mud huts with conical roofs that were all whitewashed. p. 561. Bab is pronounced like Bob as in Robert.

CHAPTER 3

In Aleppo, while walking through Saliba Street, my cousin Parsegh Odabashian happened to see the carriage driver as well as the little girl. The little girl recognized him and said "uncle," and he looked up and he saw that it was Victoria. The carriage driver told him everything that had happened to us on the way. Parsegh took both of them to his house and found out that Victoria's mother had gone from Katma to Kilis, so he sent the girl to her mother. We were later told that Victoria had gotten sick on the road and had died four days later.

<u>Tetif</u>: (Tefrije)

My father was in Hama and he came to Bab and found us with the help of Hama's Commissar. We realized that they were going to deport us from Bab as well. We decided to escape to a small village nearby. Next to Bab, there was a small village called Tetif. We arranged for an Arab to take us there. He came one night and took us to his village of Tetif. He rented us a room from his house and we paid him rent. We spent the winter over there, but that winter I got very sick. Fortunately, I recovered.

In the meantime, my father had made friends with the four important people of Tetif and for the time being we were safe. The gendarmes never came knocking at our door, but illness spread so rapidly that Armenians were dying by the thousands. The villagers became infected as well and they also started dying, including the four well-known people we had gotten to know. Once again we were left alone with no one to help us.

<u>Aramig in Tetif (Tefrije):</u>

One day we saw that five people from the government had come to our village. They said they were going to build a hospital for the deportees. One of them was a doctor, an Armenian by the name of Vahan Emirhanian. He pulled me aside and said, "Don't stay here; escape to somewhere else." He was concerned that we may contract some infection from the sick soldiers.[34] *My youngest brother, Aramig was three and a half years old; he got sick and died while we were in Tetif. My father and I dug a grave site for him; we said the Lord's Prayer and buried him. Saying is very easy but the memory of the event stays with you forever.*

Tilling the Land

Fertile lands, next to Euphrates
Being tilled by an Arab *fallah (peasant)*.

Do not go deep with your plow
Lest you hit against
The bones of our ancestors that are buried there.
Last drop of blood they shed
Enriched these sacred lands.
     (Chorus) *Der Voghormia, Der Voghormia.*
      (God Have Mercy on Us)

Ladies in Constantinople having tea
With their fingers curled around
Tulip shaped clear glass tea cups
Talking about the weather.

Are there small bones of infants and newborns?
Their necks cut easily with scimitars
Designed for that purpose
Left from *Janissary* days of the Turks,
(Having been abducted from Christian homes

---

[34] There was a common rumor that the Turkish government was transferring the soldiers with venereal diseases towards the Syrian Desert route towards Deir el-Zor, to expose the Arab population which had revolted against Turkish colonization. Vahan Emirhanian is also mentioned in Sarkissian, K. *My Memories of Seventy Years.* p. 577.

CHAPTER 3

In early childhood and trained as ruthless killing machines.)
                    (Chorus) *Der Voghormia, DerVoghormia.*

Ladies in Istanbul having tea
With their fingers curled around
Tulip shaped clear glass teacups
Talking about the latest styles.

Wearing antique gold pendent
Given by her husband
Whose Turkish family, after the war
Gotten suddenly wealthy.

God was astounded in his heaven
When he saw the writing in Armenian
Back of the pendent:
"May God be my witness,
I will love you forever."

Fertile lands next to Euphrates
Being tilled by an Arab *fallah*.

                    (Chorus) *Der Voghormia, Der Voghormia.*
                                        Gregory Ketabgian 2010

GM: Your youngest brother, what did he die from and how old was he?
AK: Three and half years old. He was not hungry, but he was sick. He used to drink water from different places. He was sick from early childhood. The doctors had told us that he should drink goat's milk since the mother's milk was too heavy for him. When he was one year old in Kayseri, we bought a goat to provide him the milk. He was a very smart boy, smarter than I was.
GM: He was with you then, during the deportation.
AK: Yes.
GM: Did he walk or was he being carried?
AK: I had rented 7 donkeys,....

Of Lice, Typhus and Death

"The lice were so numerous that they formed a line like ants as they travelled between the tents. We had not bathed for months since we had left Gesaria. We would pick up the lice off of our bodies; but the only way to kill them was by burning them or throwing them in a bottle of alcohol. The well-fed lice would make a popping sound when they burned. Some people would burn twigs, branches and dry grass on the ground where they would be pitching their tent to get rid of the lice, but within a day or two the lice from the neighboring tents would migrate on over."

When my father woke up after being unconscious, due to high fever and dehydration, he found that his baby brother, Aramig had died and his mother was close to death. They buried Aramig by the side of the road. But he had mentioned that they were not able to find an Armenian priest to give the last rites. Most of the Armenian priests were killed early during the march, after being subjected to great atrocities.

My father and his brothers brought their mother back to life by feeding her small amounts of fluid with a medicine dropper. She was a woman of small stature with a pleasant personality. In addition to calling her Arous Ana, the grandchildren affectionately would call her *Kuchuk Ana* (Little Grandmother), because of her size. Early on, her mother, our great-grandmother Benlian was still alive and she was the Great Grandmother.

* * *

My grandmother's sole purpose in life appeared to be to protect and nourish her grandchildren. She made sure that we were dressed warmly even during the summer months and made sure we did not sit in a draft. She did not want me to jump very high while playing games, in fear that my "spleen would fall down" or my "liver would come to my throat." She was trying to protect and nourish

CHAPTER 3

My grandmother Arousiag Kitabjian, "Arous Ana".
Picture from Beirut, Lebanon in the mid-1950s.

the future generation in the only way she knew. I am convinced, having lost her only daughter Hranoush as well as Aramig, the baby of the family, she was determined to protect us from harm.

Once I was fascinated by a printing-press that had a facility in a walled section of town called *Hokedoon* (House of Spirit), which was a safe and gated resting area that was used in the past by Christian pilgrims on their way to Jerusalem and later to help the new arrivals from the Northern provinces who were deported during the Genocide. I was only about seven years old and was returning from school, but had lost track of time. I was fascinated by the machinery with the hand-fed printer and the way it moved when the man pushed a pedal. My entire family was apparently involved in searching for me. My grandmother found me watching the printer take out the printed page and put in a new sheet of paper. The machine would turn over and print the new page, one page at a time.

As children, we always wanted to sleep over at her place, because she would cook us special favorites and at times she would pick me up from kindergarten, take me to her home close by and feed me *"manti"* in broth, among other favorites and would circle around me while I was eating and would say in Turkish, "Are you eating? Good, eat, eat!"

My grandmother spoke only Turkish, since while she was growing up in Gesaria, she was forbidden to speak any Armenian by the Ottoman Emperor Sultan Hamid, and the punishment, if caught, was to have her tongue cut out.

She had taught me a short poem about a cake. When asked to recite a poem in kindergarten at Haigazian School, I raised my hand. When I started the recitation, to my surprise everyone started laughing, and the teacher quickly shut me up and had me sit down. The poem was in Turkish and for that reason a taboo in any Armenian school in Aleppo. At the entrance of the school there was an inscription on the top of the arch prohibiting us to utter any words of the "enemy." That incident affected me throughout my life and I became reluctant to speak up in class, unless I knew my subject matter well.

*   *   *

While on our trip through Historic Armenia, we had gone into a dry goods store to buy some dried fruit. While I was speaking to the grocer, he looked up with a surprised facial expression. I asked in Turkish if he understood me. He said that he understood, but I was speaking ancient Turkish. Then it struck me that I had learned my Turkish from my grandmother and had not used it much since then. Meanwhile Turks had made a great effort in modernizing and Turkifying their language since previously it contained a lot of

Arabic words. My Turkish had remained as it was, ancient, almost hundred years old.

Meskene to Abu Harrara: Father describes further atrocities on the route:

> *Summer came and they drove us to Meskene and then to Abu Harrara (Abuharar).* We arrived at Abu Harrara in the desert with incredible difficulties. It was a police station. There was a corporal; his name was Rahmeddin. He had ten gendarmes with him. I can say that he made all Armenians suffer a great deal. He was a beast who had no pity.

GM: What was the name of the short person in the railroad station who killed a lot of Armenians?
AK: Rahmeddin Onbashi.
GM: Can you tell me about him?
AK: He was a military officer, an inspector at this railroad station. He had become powerful at the time of the deportations. He was brutal; I can say that he killed a large number of people by crushing them with his boots. We were trying to make a living; I was selling soap imported from Aleppo. I used to get a bag of soap and arranged the bars in front of me to sell to the women, mostly Armenians and some Arabs; they used to cross the river and come to buy them. I used to make a few *gurushes* (cents) each day by selling the soap. One day he came and hit an Armenian and killed him with his boots. However by taking money from us, he kept us in a cleared field that contained 500 Armenian tents. If he had not kept us there, we would have been in Markadeh and Sheddadiye.[35]
GM: In the massacres?
AK: Yes, in the middle of it all.

---

[35] Markadeh (Marqada) and Sheddadiye (Shaddadeh) were the killing fields near Deir el-Zor. Sun bleached bone fragments of the victims are close to the surface and can be easily obtained. A monument to all the Genocide victims was erected at Markadeh in 1990.

LEAVING KAYSERI

GM: He did this not because he wanted to help you, but for the money?
AK: Yes, we were saved because of the money.

My Sister Hranoush in Abu Harrara:

We stayed in Abu Harrara for four to five months. I was 18 years old. My sister Hranoush was two years younger than me and she got sick in Abu Harrara and died. We were lucky we found a priest and we buried her. We continued on with our march. We faced many difficulties. Only the person who has marched that perilous road knows what it was like.

They wouldn't let us stay in one place for long. They were constantly driving us out. We were always trying to stay back as much as possible, because the people who had gone before us, some of them escaped and they would come and tell us to try not to go because they had witnessed the killing of all the previous deportees. But there was not much we could do beyond paying the gendarmes and staying behind.

The Arab in the Syrian Desert

A row of oxcarts was making its way slowly in the hot summer sun on the Syrian Desert towards Rakka and Deir el-Zor. My father was driving the oxcart. He had his mother in the cart with him, the bedding and a few possessions, while his father and the other boys were walking. They came to an area where they were building a structure. An Arab with his head gear and Arab *burnuz* (long cloak or tunic) was motioning to them. When they got closer to him, he said in Turkish, "Bring your cart behind this wall, since all the others that are going towards Deir el-Zor are being killed."

CHAPTER 3

* * *

Fast forward to Aleppo, 1945, on a weekend, father rented a car with a driver to take us to Jarablus. This was a small town northeast of Aleppo on the Euphrates River, at the Syrian-Turkish border. Here, the train from Baghdad to Istanbul crossed the river over a steel bridge. We went to visit a good friend of my father's from the past, Mr. Levon Gerboyan. They used to visit each other often when Mr. Gerboyan came to town for supplies. He used to run a garage, auto repair shop, grocery store and a café all in one, at Jarablus. As children, we had no idea what had bonded them in the past. I clearly remember the small village with unpaved streets and the courtyard of their home. It was also unpaved and had made it convenient for us to play marbles on it.

We went to play on the edge of the Euphrates River and I still remember the flat, black pebbles and wondered if they were volcanic rocks that had washed downriver from the Armenian mountains. On the northern bank of the river above the hills, we could see Turkish soldiers guarding the border.

Once or twice a year, Mr. Gerboyan would send a good sized fish caught in the Euphrates River, packed in ice. My mother always hated the sight of it since she had to clean the scales and the insides, before she could cook it. The fishy smell persisted in spite of all her efforts. We did not get to eat much fish otherwise, since there was no proper refrigeration in Aleppo at that time.

* * *

My father and grandfather, together with the other family members stayed on the construction site for a few months, working and picking up telephone poles. They got their groceries from Bilezikji Enver, who after befriending them had told them, "Don't tell anyone, but I am also Armenian."

LEAVING KAYSERI

The Arab in the Syrian Desert was an Armenian!

* * *

Mr. Gerboyan's son and daughter came and located my office in Pasadena for their and their families' medical care. Mr. Gerboyan's daughter called once concerning an infant niece of theirs who had recurrent fever with vomiting, abdominal pain and diarrhea. She had been worked up repeatedly at UCLA Medical center for septicemia and complete gastrointestinal evaluation that had turned out to be negative. I entertained the possibility of Familial Mediterranean Fever (FMF). Since the expert in that field was Dr. Schwartz at UCLA, I referred her there.

Some twenty years later, I had a young woman come to see me in the office for evaluation before marriage, "Do you know who I am? When I was an infant, you diagnosed my FMF and I was placed on the correct medical management by Dr. Schwartz; I have done well since then. I thank you very much."

Rakka: My father recounts how they were saved once more:

One day, the news came that all the people deported before us had been killed and they were waiting for more people to come. They chased us from Abu Harrara to the opposite bank of the Euphrates River to Rakka. On this side, there was an officer responsible for ten gendarmes.

There were about a hundred Armenians in our group, and they dropped off our caravan there. My father went out of our tent to see the officer. When he came back, he said that one of the officer's helpers was an Armenian from Gesaria, a grocer named Hagop, who remembered him.

CHAPTER 3

> *Two days later, they said that all the newcomers were going to be leaving the next day. My father went to see Hagop Aga as a brother and asked him, "What do you think about us?" He said: "I already talked to the officer; you will be moving from your tent to ours tonight, and you should not leave our tent until the caravan leaves. You can move back to your tent later." I can say that this Hagop Aga saved our family. This time we had gotten off cheap. The officer's legs were hurting because of the humidity. He asked for two pairs of woolen stockings and we presented them to him. We stayed there for a few months.*

Taxicab Driver in Istanbul

We were in a yellow taxicab travelling up a hilly street in Istanbul towards the Baghlarbashi Armenian Cemetery in the Uskudar section of Istanbul. There were six of us tourists visiting some Armenian sites, after returning from an emotionally charged pilgrimage to eastern Turkey during the summer of 2006. We were talking in English and occasionally in Armenian.

All of a sudden the taxicab driver asked us about what language we were speaking. When he found out that we were Armenian, he said he was a Kurd and he had a number of cousins who had an Armenian mother. Then he started telling us all about his old aunt who was found in his uncle's garden behind his house in Diyarbekir. She was hiding from the Turks with her newborn child in her arms in 1915. He said, "We know all about the massacres and the Turks know it as well, but they do not want to admit it. Now they are trying to do the same thing to us."

Zeyarat: Father explains about work delaying his deportation toward Deir el-Zor:

Picture taken during the preparation of *harrisah* in the historic church courtyard in Bitias[36] in 1930. My father is the third person (with a fez) from the left holding on to my sister Arpiné (4 years old). Mr. Gerboyan is the 6th person w i t h a fez, (only picture of him with my father.) My uncle Parsegh is the only other person with a fez to his left. The person in the center pointing to the herisa is my Uncle Haig.

On the south side of the Euphrates River, across from Rakka, the new caravans brought lots of people. Half the people would go toward Deir el-Zor and the other half would remain there. There were some sheiks' homes on the south side of Rakka named Zeyarat. One day it was decided by the government that a military base would be built there. A director came and said that whoever wants to work to build the garrison, should come and register their names. He said that in return for their work, they would be compensated with wheat. The majority of the

---

[36] Bitias was in the northwestern part of Syria near the Mediterranean, south of the Turkish border which was drawn after the end of WWI and was under the French mandate. It was a beautiful section of the country with lots of lush vegetation and pleasant Mediterranean climate and my parents among other Armenians used to go there for summer vacation. But it was given back to the Turks in 1938 by France to appease them and keep them from joining Germany during the ensuing WWII. Its Armenian residents were uprooted for a second time and forced to immigrate to Syria and Lebanon. Apparently *Harrisah*, which is hurled wheat that is cooked with fowl until it becomes pasty, was served in large pots or boilers as can be seen in the picture against the church wall. There were seven pots, one for each of the seven villages in the region. The villages were Yogunoluk, Bitias, Kebusiye, Hidirbey, Hacihabipli, Aziv and Vakifli.

CHAPTER 3

people registered because we were all hungry and we knew that we were going to stay there until we finished building the garrison. If they gave you your daily bread, wouldn't you go? When we talked to Hagop Aga he told us that it was a good idea to go there. "The director told me so," he said.

We went to Zeyarat. Molds were made for the purpose of making bricks and scaffoldings were set up. We started working. My hands got swollen from carrying the blocks. I thought that I should find an easier job because this job was too tough for me. One night I made a few whistles out of tin. I presented them to the gendarmes. I told them that I would make more whistles for the night watchmen. They told me, "Don't go to the construction job, we want you to make whistles."

In the meantime my father said, "I am going to go to the tent of the officer in charge of the camp and will talk to him." There was a gendarme standing at the entrance of the tent and we had become friends with him. He let my father enter the tent and saluted him. "What do you want?" the officer asked him, "I am a jeweler, effendi, do you still want me to work in this mud?" he asked. The director answered, "Come and sit here next to me and let me see." The director removed a gemstone from his pocket. "Take a look at this," he said. My father removed his magnifying glass from his pocket and after examining the stone, he said, "These are artificial stones." "You know it very well. I am going to give you a job where you have to pay very close attention. I want to make you a supervisor over these people who are working here. However, if you don't supervise them well, then you will be responsible. Can you do it?" My father said, "Yes."

The officer said, "Get up and come with me." He took my father to the workplace. He stopped all the workers and said to them, "Look, this is Master Krikor; he is going to be your supervisor; all of you should obey him. If you need anything, you talk to him and he will let me know." In this manner my father had been saved from working in the mud.

As for me, I became friends with the gendarmes. They put me in charge of the watchmen. I would walk by them to prevent them from falling asleep. They had two groups of watchmen who would alternate their hours with each other so the entire 24 hours was covered.

They laid the foundation of the garrison. They installed the doors and the windows. We were waiting for some wooden posts from Barajek or from Jarablus to cover the top of the building. We waited for a while; it didn't arrive. But while we were working, we saw many caravans coming and passing us up and going toward Deir el-Zor. For the time being we had been safe here. Finally the caravans stopped coming. The wood to cover the top of the building never arrived.

The Visitor[37]

Please, everyone.
Come in from the bright sun.
Gather together for a short talk
In front of that map.

Right inside the entrance,
It is much cooler.
You will see a map with arrows.
What are the red dots, you ask?

---

[37] This poem's voice is of an outsider acting as a Genocide Museum docent taking a class of students on a tour of the museum.

CHAPTER 3

What does red color represent?
Anyone?
Yes, it could be color of a fruit.
Pomegranates?
Watermelons! (You jest.)
Yes, color on a flag.

Could it be the color of
Freshly spilled blood?

As you have noticed,
Some of the circles are bigger than others.
Red is the color of blood shed
By the innocents in those lands.

Could the size of the circles indicate
The severity of the crime?

The arrows indicate
The direction deportees were driven
With whips and bayonets of the gendarmes.
Very good observation!
Yes, the route continues into the Syrian Desert.
You ask, was it very hot and sandy there?

Yes, all marches into the desert start in April
When it is cool, but the incessant summer sun follows
And, for some, the march ends early.

And the route follows the right bank of Euphrates River.
Were they allowed to drink from the river, you ask?
Anyone?

LEAVING KAYSERI

Thirst and starvation kills people easily,
Without wasting any bullets,
Less manual work involved.
The young, the sick and elderly
Succumb!

I wonder who colored the Euphrates blue.

Why do I ask that, you say?
Blue, the color of our rivers and lakes,
And the freedom of the blue sky.

Correct!
Blue, second color on the flag,
Below the red, but easily tainted
By blood.

The river ran red during the height of deportations;
Many freshly slaughtered bodies were thrown in.

Next, let us move on to another area,
Where there are three somber men in fezzes.
Who do you think they are?

Yes, they are the three men
They were the instigators and leaders.

And how about the next exhibit of young men?
Anyone?

Well, I will tell you, but do not forget;
They are the men who, in retribution,
Assassinated the leaders, after the war.

Do you think they got our lands back?
Did they bring back all the people
Who were slaughtered on the way?
Babies with their mothers

Drowned in all the lakes and rivers?

I agree! Vengeance does not justify the crime,
Instead it engenders hatred all over again.

Oh my! Here come the guards to evict me again.

They do not agree with some of my viewpoints.

We have so much to discuss yet.

We did not cover the last color on the flag?

It is officially orange, but to me it looks more like
The color of ripe apricots.
It signifies our homeland, our orchards and vineyards
That gave us sweet fruit in the summer
And jam and dried fruits for the cold winters.
Yes, officer, I am leaving.

Listen, everyone!
Do you promise
To plant an apricot tree in your yard
For this summer?

Here are some choice seeds.
(Prunus armeniaca.)
Gregory Ketabgian 2009

Picnic at Abughalghal

The Boyamians, Stepan and Krikor, were two orphaned cousins

from Zeitoon[38] who had become truck drivers. They wanted to settle down in Aleppo to establish a business and start their families. My father found a Dunlop Tire agency for them and they rented a space next to my father's store, which was located below Hotel Carlton in Bustan Keleb.

The Boyamians were husky, muscular men with deep voices, but they were gentle in nature. They allowed me to go inside their store and run my hands over the brand new tires on display with their intricate ridges and let me smell the fresh tires. They would frequently come to my father for advice and discussion on varied matters which included even some jokes and gossip.

One day, it was decided that our families would get together and go on a picnic along the Euphrates River. Abughalghal was a rock strewn area on the edge of the turbulent Euphrates, on the way to Quamichli on the North Eastern part of Syria. The bus

At last the bus has arrived at the Abughalghal picnic site.

---

[38] Only 7 members of the Boyamian family survived when they arrived in Deir el-Zor out of the 46 that left Zeytoon during the early stages of the Genocide. The two orphan cousins worked as porters at the Gare de Baghdad railroad station in Aleppo to survive. Later they became truck drivers for 10 years, bringing asphalt from Homs for the French forces. (From Zaven Boyamian, personal communication)

driver was one of the Boyamian cousins. It took us four hours to get there over mostly dirt roads. The inside of the bus was hot and dusty. The place was isolated but wooded, shady and beautiful, which was a rare find for that part of the country. As soon as the food preparation had gotten under way, it was realized that we had already exhausted most of our water supply. The muddy Euphrates River was flowing very swiftly among rocky passages and seemed too dangerous for us to approach.

Throughout the long march in the desert during the Genocide, this was the stretch of Euphrates where people committed suicide. Having lost all hope and seeing no end to the sickness, starvation, and the death of their infants and other family members, they would commit suicide, sometimes with their infants in their arms. Other women, who had been raped repeatedly by the Turkish soldiers or Kurds and were unwilling to bear a Muslim's child, would prefer death instead. My father would relate that usually in the early evening hours, one would hear some woman with her infant in her arms, or an older man run towards the river through the crowd screaming and would jump in without any hesitation.

Was this just another picnic in the wilderness, or did it have additional significance to those members in the group who had survived the deportation along this river, the starvation, the illnesses and the killings? Thirty-five years had passed since the beginning of the Genocide.

The Boyamians had also invited their priest, who had similarly survived the deportation from Zeytoon. He was gracious enough to bless the food prepared for the picnic lunch with all of us present, as well as the holy ground where numerous Armenian "*nahadags*" (martyrs) had perished.

My father remembered that during their march along the Euphrates, the Turkish gendarmes had not allowed them to get too close to the river. He had learned that if you would dig the sandy region two to three feet deep, you could get clean filtered drinking water. A small ditch was dug with the tire iron and shovel in the bus, and we had cool, clear water for all the members of the party.

Handful of Grass

Looking for a handful of grass
In the Syrian Desert
After the rains
To satisfy the gnawing hunger
Always present.

Your granddaughter
Pointing at the lawn,
While in her playground
In disbelief;
"Did Papa eat this grass?"

Digging furiously in total darkness
Next to the Euphrates,
"Another foot down!"
With our hands bleeding,
Sharp rocks.

"Get to the water level!"
To drink with abandon
Like raw sex,
Disregard sediment and worms.
Rusted tin cans
Sharp edges,
Salvaged and kept
Like silver chalices.

Muddy Euphrates

CHAPTER 3

Flowing furiously,
Picnicking with family
Surviving Zeitoontsy orphans
While their elderly priest prays;
"Astvatz Bahbane" (God Protect)
Pointing to the ground
As if souls were present there.

Relieve hunger and thirst
In the hands of gendarmes
Goal for survival.
Not able to think
Whether God was present
To punish the evil men.

What sins had we committed,
How many prayers did we have to offer?
Were we being tested for
Steadfastness of our faith
Which almost killed us all off?

We are the grandchildren of Noah,
We always thought we were the chosen race,
Rainbow of peace, as a Covenant,
On the eastern side of Ararat.
Eternally protected.

But wait.
Syrian Desert flooded
With Armenian blood!

Was Noah Christian?
Were we praying to the wrong gods?

LEAVING KAYSERI

Where are Aramazt, Vahagn, Mihr, Anahid?[39]
Even now, facing denial
We need self-reliance,
We need power like Sasoontzi Tavit.[40]

                        Gregory Ketabgian 2010

Working on the Abughalghal water site.

---

[39] Pre-Christian pagan gods of Armenians. Aramazd: all powerful god, father of all creators. Vahagn: god of power, war and victory. Anahid: god of motherhood, fertility, healing and wisdom. Mihr: god of light, harmony and advice.

[40] Sasoontzy Tavit, from the epic poem named "*Daredevils of Sasoon*" (English version by Leon Surmelian, 1964), generations of powerful heroes protecting the Armenian population against invaders.

CHAPTER 3

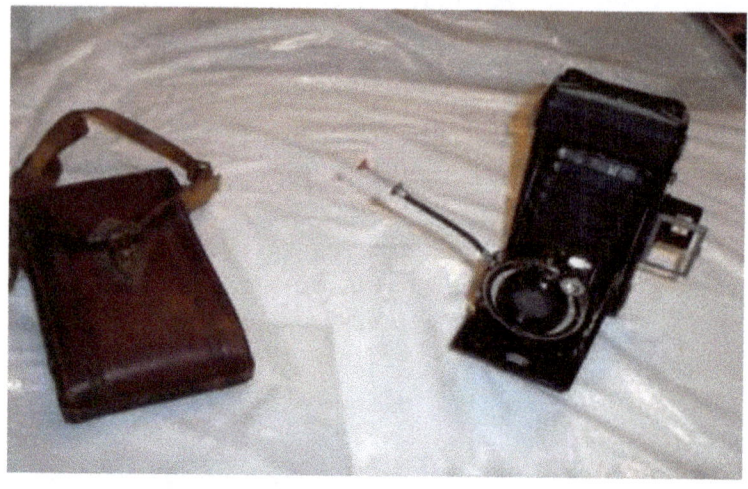

My father's Zeiss Ikon collapsible 120mm camera with which most of the pictures were taken

Chapter 4

On the Way to Deir el-Zor: Sebka: My father continues on his challenging journey:

> One day an inspector by the name of Haka Bey (Hakki Bey) [41] came. He had come back all the way from Baghdad. He was checking how many deportees remained alive on the roads. He was on his way to Aleppo. A month later we received orders instructing us that all the Armenians scattered on the roads had to go to the other side of the bridge to Deir el-Zor.
>
> We were among the nineteen hundred people from Aleppo on their way to Deir el-Zor. They gathered us and sent us to Sebka, where they put us in a barn. Until then, all the Armenians who had gone through there ahead of us had been massacred. They were waiting for orders from someone in the government headquarters to decide what to do with us. We got to rest there a little bit.
>
> There was a town crier who was announcing in Turkish that the order had come: "Tomorrow morning you are going toward Deir el-Zor, however, since you don't have any animals, you will be walking. You can take with you what you can carry of your belongings."
>
> When the people heard this, they started screaming and crying. There was weeping and gnashing of teeth. We

---

[41] Hakki Bey was dispatched in August of 1916 by central authorities as "inspector general" of *Sevkiyet* (Deportations) and was brutal in uprooting orphans and other stragglers on the Euphrates line to be deported to Deir el-Zor to be killed. Kevorkian, Raymond. p. 656, 661.

CHAPTER 4

felt as if we were in hell. We went crazy.[42] *These events were not according to God's intent. We lost whatever faith we had.*

When the town crier finished what he had to say, the gendarmes ordered us to get out of Sebka.

There was a guard who was standing by the gate of the barn who would not let people get back in. Kevork Sapsezian was a goldsmith from Marash whose wife was very ill with a high fever. She was unaware of what was happening. As they were walking out of the barn, because the ground was uneven, she tripped and fell. There was a gendarme on horseback who shouted, "Why are you blocking the way!" He rode back and forth over the fallen woman. Sapsezian's wife died on the spot. The husband stood there, frozen. The gendarme said, "What are you waiting for? Walk!" He left the dead wife there. He had two boys and two girls who walked in front of him. My father took the man's arm and we started walking. That's how we left Sebka and continued on our journey.

Holding on to whatever they could carry, the people started marching on the right bank of the Euphrates River. A few meters away, they had these boats with holes in them. These were what took us across the river to the left bank.
The desert was on one side and the Euphrates River was on the other side.

We walked for four hours. Sapsezian's face turned pale and he was unable to walk. He told my father, "If we reach where the water separates, I am going to hide there. I will rest there until sunrise and will follow you. If I don't follow you and come back, don't look for me. I trust my four children

---

[42] Being sent to Deir el-Zor and crossing the river usually was preliminary to being sent to the killing fields.

to you." He separated from us and left. We never saw him again.

Merat Nahiye:

There were lots of people who died at Merat Nahiye. His three children died there also. Only one of his two daughters survived.

While we were in Merat Nahiya, my grandmother had sent us ten gold Osmanian (Ottoman) pieces through the post office. We had the papers to pick them up. The next day we promised two majits (silver coins) to a policeman. My father went to the post office with the police officer to whom he had promised the money and brought the gold pieces home. It was amazing that they would give the money to us. Now we were wealthy. After giving the ten gold pieces, the man at the post office said to my father, "Let me see, there is more money from Konya in your name." Wrapped in a piece of cloth were five majits and he gave that to my father as well. We had written a letter to some relatives in Konya during our difficult days.[43]

A few days later, the commissar of the city and a few other people came to the bridge and read our names. We started walking across the bridge. My father was able to carry my mother. His money belt and our stomachs were full and we were happy.

AK: At the time my mother was half dead. Later, when the 14 families were going to be taken into Deir el-Zor, while we were walking on the bridge to cross over the river, the commissar asked my father, "What is that thing you are carrying on your back, a

---

[43] Sarkissian, K.p. 568. Money transfers were initially set up through Agricultural Bank for farmers to get seed money, but later were used for money transfers for the general population.

monkey or what?" Because she had lice, we had cut her hair short so she no longer looked like a human being. "No," my father said, "It is my wife." "Where are you taking her?" He asked. "To Deir el-Zor," my father replied. "Throw her in the water and I will get you a beautiful girl," he said. "In our religion that is not allowed; I have promised to take care of her until death, in the best way I can."

GM: The man said, "Throw her over and I will get you another wife?"

AK: Yes, we are right on the bridge, if we throw her over, she goes. And the Euphrates River there was narrow, very deep and was flowing with great force.

GM: So did your mother survive?

AK: My mother survived until age 93. My father was 57 years old when we came from Deir el-Zor. For 9 to 10 years he worked in Aleppo. He had a cerebral hemorrhage and he died in three days. My mother lived for another 50 years.

GM: Fifty years?

AK: Yes, yes. It has been 4 or 5 years since she has passed away. She was 93 years old.

GM: It is a sad story.

AK: Oh! Wherever you turn, it is a sad story.

My Grandfather Krikor Kitabjian and my Grandmother Arous Ana (1928.)

LEAVING KAYSERI

Arous Ana

My Gesaratsi (from Kayseri) grandmother was a small-statured woman who wore black since my grandfather Krikor had passed away before I was born. I was named after him.

"Krikor, go see what your grandmother has brought, so we can continue the class," said my teacher at Gertasiratz Armenian Elementary School. The school was conducted in one of the old Arab homes in Aleppo that had multiple rooms around a courtyard. Whenever anyone entered the courtyard, they would be noticed from every classroom window.

My grandmother would bring a package filled with raisins, bananas, and French pastry about every two weeks or so, in spite my telling her not to do it. She would come into the courtyard and would wait until I came to pick it up. She would admonish me that I should eat it all and not give it to the others. My classmates would wait until recess time for me to open the package and essentially would finish it before I would have a chance to taste any of its contents.

My grandmother was the same woman, who as a skeleton my grandfather was carrying on his back in the Syrian Desert over a bridge on the Euphrates River to enter Deir el-Zor.

Merod (Marat): Father recounts hunger and starvation:

> *After thirteen days of walking and marching, we arrived across from the entrance to the town of Deir el-Zor. A doctor came and examined us. When he found out that we had no money, he left and declared that we were sick. They took us to the village of Merod, which was one hour south of the Deir el-Zor bridge. They put us in barns and stables. We were the last group. We stayed there for three months.*

CHAPTER 4

Now from 1800, there were only 750 of us left. We were five in our family and we didn't have any losses there. We were very sick and hungry. If this had gone on for another month, none of us would have survived.

The Golden Tooth[44]

While on the road to Deir el-Zor in a camp close to a Chechen village, my grandfather Krikor found a job in that village piercing ears and making earrings from silver wire. But the income which was bartered by the villagers for food was not enough to keep the whole family fed satisfactorily. By now they had used up all their money, and had sold all of their possessions.

One day my father Artin told his mother, "Wouldn't it be nice to have some *ghatmer* (layered dough pastry) right now? I would do anything for it." His mother told him that they had no flour or fat to cook it with. But seeing how hungry they were, she said, "The only possession I have is my golden tooth; I want you to pull it out and sell it." He refused to do so initially, but after repeated requests from his mother, he pulled the golden crown and sold it to get the necessary supplies.

* * *

Fast forward to Aleppo 1920, they had left Deir el-Zor and had gotten established and started working in Aleppo as goldsmiths. One day my father said to his mother, Arous Ana, "We are going to the dentist. You gave us your golden tooth. It helped us survive; now we have enough money to get a new one made for you."

---

[44] This story was told to Araxy Kitabjian, my cousin, Krikor Parsegh Kitabjian's wife, by my grandmother while living with them in Beirut, Lebanon.

LEAVING KAYSERI

Deir el-Zor Bridge:

They took fourteen families who were professionals to Deir el-Zor. They sent the rest to another village. All fourteen families started walking towards the bridge. My mother was very sick at this time and unable to walk. My father was carrying her on his back. The three brothers, Artin, Parsegh and Haig were walking carrying whatever was left of our belongings.

This was a caravan of one hundred-fifty people. We kept on walking. After walking for half an hour, we stopped to rest. I looked back and I couldn't see either my mother or my father. I wondered what I could do. I immediately found this young man in the caravan and I told him that I'd give him two ghurushes if he would carry my mother to the bridge. If we hadn't gone back right away, the Arabs would have killed both of my parents. The young man told me that he expected to be paid the minute he put my mother on the ground.

I didn't have a single centime in my pocket. While I was walking, I was thinking of what I was going to do. All this time I was showing my vest pocket to the man telling him, "This is where the money is," pretending that the money was ready.

I found my father. He was tired. He had put my mother down to rest, but he couldn't pick her up again. They were sitting there and crying. When my father saw me, it was as if a new life and vigor had come to him. He stood up and started praying. And I asked my father, "Can you walk?" He said, "Yes." We put my mother on the back of this fellow and we walked all the way to the bridge.

The caravan had reached the bridge as well. The young man put my mother down. He wanted the two gurushes so

CHAPTER 4

he could buy some bread. From our belongings, I picked out a few things; I quickly sold them and gave the man his money. We spent the rest of the money to get food for us. That night we all had a restful sleep.

Finally, we arrived at the town square by the palace in Deir el-Zor. We were told, "You should look into what you may want to do for a living."

The Pocket Knife

Recently found
Your ivory covered knife
At the bottom of your toolbox
With other rusted old tools

Ever present pocket knife
Accompanied with magnifying lens,
Having saved you and your family's life.
Showing Deir el-Zor Kurd,
Carving floral designs on silver bracelets.

Worn out blades, rusted,
Not used for decades.
Still holds memories of peeling oranges
On mountain tops,
Opening cans,
Peeling cucumbers at picnics.

"Proper tools in capable hands
Makes the Artisan proud" you had said.

Gregory Ketabgian 2009

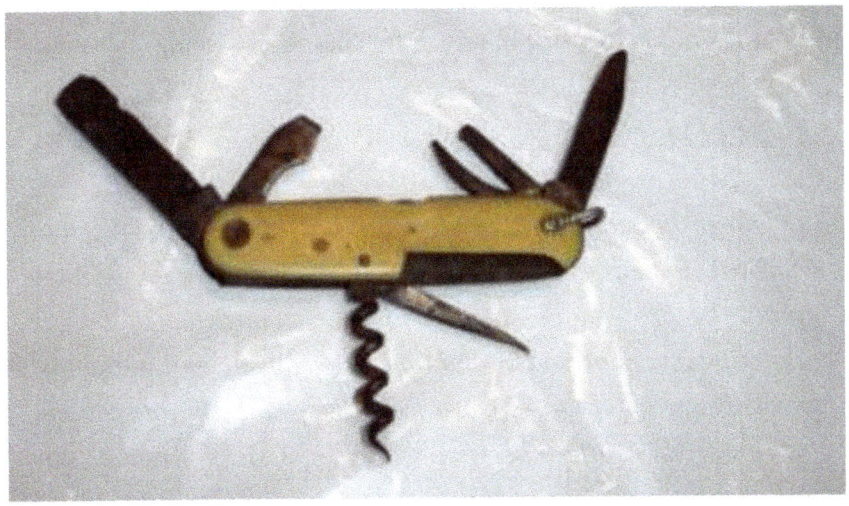

Deir el-Zor Kurds

Deir el-Zor Arabs would not allow the Armenians into town since they were known to harbor disease. They were kept in a tent city outside of town, across from the Euphrates River.

My father noticed a Kurd silversmith selling heavy silver bracelets and anklets with rudimentary etchings on them. Arab and Kurd women wore their wealth on their bodies in the form of silver and gold jewelry. My father talked to the jeweler and told him that he and his father could do even more elaborate etchings and decorations. He had learned the technique by having spent hours watching his father and his two uncles work on gold and silver. They used to do their jewelry work at home in Gesaria and were somewhat secretive of their technique. The store was used mainly for display and sales. One uncle, who was an expert in silver and gold relief work, was so secretive about his technique that he would go to another room to do his work, away from the other members of the family.

My father took his ever present pocket knife and small magnifying lens from his pocked and showed the Kurd some

CHAPTER 4

examples that he had watched his father and uncles create back home in Gesaria. The Kurd was impressed and invited the whole family to his home to work in return for their daily food.

Working in Deir el-Zor: My father describes...

> *Our profession was that of goldsmith, therefore a goldsmith came and took us to his house and gave us a room. As we were guests, he brought us some food which consisted of bulgur pilaf, five pieces of bread, and onions. I can say that in the last two years we had not eaten a meal like that. My father said, "Let's eat very little otherwise we will get sick." We ate little amounts for a few days. Our travel ended here and we started working.*
>
> *Previously while staying in Abu Harrara for three or four months, the government was asking for the deportees to pick up the fallen telephone poles. We met Chechen Abu Ibrahim Chavoush and invited him to our tent. We offered him some food and coffee. We became friends. He said, "I don't want you to go to Deir el-Zor, but if you do, make sure to look for me. Everyone in Deir el-Zor knows who I am and I will try and help you as much as I can. A relative of mine is a goldsmith and I will see to it that you can work with him," he said.*
>
> *My father worked at the house where we had pilaf for a few days, but we found out that this man didn't have enough work for us all. I went to look for Ibrahim Chavoush. I found him. He took me to his relative's house where I saw that they had plenty of work. I started working there for lunch and one gurush a day. I worked there for a month.*
>
> *Through Chechen Ibrahim Effendi Chavoush, we met Hassan and Yacoub, who my father and I made friends with. We were going to share half of the money we made with them. Thus we started working. We found out that all the goldsmiths were busy, but we were scared to work on gold jewelry because we thought*

that we could harm their business by taking it over.

We worked for a while, I don't know if we worked for weeks or months because we had lost track of time; but we were earning money.[45] *One day Ibrahim Chavoush got sick. From what I know, he had pneumonia. He called me. He had high fever. "These guys don't know anything," he said. He asked me to do cupping of blood, a home remedy. I helped in other ways also. After that the man got well. He told me that if I weren't there, he would have died.*

Near Death Experiences

Before antibiotics were discovered, my father had a near death experience in 1930 after having come to Aleppo from Deir el-Zor. He had gone to El Kulliyeh Hospital at AUB to have an elective tonsillectomy. He had gone there because it had a better reputation than the hospitals in Aleppo and had the latest innovations in medicine. It was a teaching hospital and had American-trained staff. This was after he had experienced frequent sinus infections.

He describes having the tonsillectomy without any incident, but after the anesthesia wore off, he started vomiting blood in spite of swallowing ice chips. The doctors took him back to surgery, but they were unable to stop his bleeding. They might have nicked the carotid artery, which is right behind the tonsils. If the tonsils were retracted too forcibly, it would bring the artery forward and it could easily be punctured. He experienced progressive weakness and dizziness and blacking out with each episode of vomiting.

Upon waking up the following morning, the next thing he remembers is that he was in bed and the bleeding had stopped. He thought he had died and come back to life. Most likely he had bled enough to lower his blood pressure for a blood clot to form.

Later he used to joke about it, saying that it must not yet have been the time for him to die. That Angel Gabriel, who was supposed

---

[45] In his UCLA interview he reports having worked in Deir el-Zohr for 19 months.

to come to claim his spirit, was looking for him in Deir el-Zor and did not find him there. He claimed that each extra day that he lived was a victory over the Turks.

A Role Model

My experience with a serious illness occurred when I was about 15 years old. I had felt some pain on my left chest region, but did not pay attention to it since I was also weightlifting. Two weeks later I developed a cough and a high fever, becoming weak and bedridden.

My parents decided to have a young, recently graduated doctor to come and check on me. After examining me briefly, he said that I had a chest infection and prescribed a large white pill (Sulfa) and aspirin to be taken every four hours. Each time I took the pills, I would feel a little more lucid and my temperature would come down, but the fever would recur and I would be lethargic again. This went on for another week. My father was very worried. He said, "We are going to lose the boy." They decided to call our previous family doctor, Dr. Salatian, who was a very kind and caring older physician with a soft touch. He came and examined me thoroughly and said that I had pneumonia. He went on to say, "I believe in treating people using the methods of both the new and the old schools of thought." Addressing my father he said, "First, you will do cupping[46] on his back, after lancing the area," showing the location of the left lower lobe area of the lungs, "to get the evil spirits out. Second, we are going to hire a nurse to stay in your house to give him Penicillin injections every 4 hours."

Actually, I felt better with the cupping right away. It felt as if some weight was lifted off my chest. Although I dreaded the aqueous

---

[46] Cupping was performed by throwing a flaming ball of cotton into a cup and then applying the cup over the skin on the area in question. The flame would go out rapidly and upon cooling the vacuum would suck the skin into the cup and, if the area was previously lanced, it would suck in the blood from that area.

Penicillin injections because they were extremely painful and were given with long needles into the buttocks, I had no choice in the matter. In ten days I was back on my feet, but very weak having lost a considerable amount of weight. I soon excused the doctor for ordering those painful injections and he became my role model for a physician.

_Mardinsi Bedros__:_ Father tells about a jeweler in Deir-el-Zor:

There was only one jeweler who was Christian, Mardinsi Bedros, who was a goldsmith but wasn't very productive. My father and I started working with Hassan and Yacoub. We did good work and when people found out and appreciated the quality of our work, they gave us their business. But we didn't know that we were taking the business away from Bedros.

Bedros would accept all the requests for customers' gold and silver work; but he was lazy. A few years passed; meanwhile he had sold many of the items the customers had left with him to be worked on, living off of it. When customers came to claim their jewelry, he had nothing to give back to them. Later we heard that he had run away from his house and hid.

Everyone was Muslim in Deir el Zor. He was the only Christian. He decided that he should drink some poison and kill himself to rid himself off of his responsibilities. Where would he buy the poison? He could buy it from the goldsmiths. He came and asked our partner, Hussein to give him some Sulemania (Nitric acid). *He said he was going to make a ring for someone and needed it for cleaning it. I didn't like the man's behavior and I told Hussein, "Don't give it to him. This man is going to drink it." But Hussein gave it to him. He took it and left.*

At midnight there was a knock at our door. When we

CHAPTER 4

opened it, Bedros fell in front of the door. We called Hussein and his older brother Hassan Effendi. They both came and took him to the hospital. When he arrived there he said, "I drank poison." They gave him the necessary treatment.

In the morning when Hassan Effendi went to the hospital, he found out that Bedros was alive. The doctor at the hospital told him, "We found this paper in his pocket." On the paper were written my and my father's names, saying that this is where he got the poison from. Thank God he didn't die and we were saved. His stomach was empty and he had vomited the poison. What a peril we were spared from!

The British Are Coming: Father is speaking...

Having lost their hope of winning the war, a month before the arrival of the British troops, the Turks had started retreating from Bagdad towards Aleppo. The officers and their wives were leaving, riding on camels. We witnessed this too. There was no government for a month. There was an officer, Fadel Effendi at Deir el-Zor and he was a good man. "Let's not say anything derogatory about the Armenians. These few people who are left here are our guests," he said.

One day we saw the British were coming from the direction of Anah (Iraq). The Arabs went to greet them. There was a garden in the middle of town. It filled up with jeeps. A commander and a sheik got out. There were close to sixty soldiers. There was a large building in the garden where they settled. All the people were happy and so were we. Because of the war, all of the goldsmiths were working in their homes. After the arrival of the British, we wanted to move our business to a store. There were lots of empty stores. We moved into one of these stores with our partners.

A few months later one of our partners said, "I am going

to work at home. If you want to, you can continue to work here." Thus we separated from our partners and continued to work. There was a time that we shared half of our earnings with our partners, but because our partners were generous, they wanted to stop doing this, saying, "Let them keep all their earnings."

Our work was very successful. For the ladies, we made bracelets and anklets; for the children, we made bracelets with bells. We never had a free day. One day, a woman came to us asking us to make a bracelet for her. We made the bracelet and gave it to her. This woman had a front tooth that was protruding out of her mouth. She asked me, "Can you fix this too? It looks very bad." I in turn asked her, "Can you stand the pain? If you can, I will cut it."

There were no dentists in town at the time. Because of the protruding tooth, her mouth was left partially open and it looked ugly. I put a pillow under the woman's head. I told her to lean on it. Goldsmiths usually have a thin saw. I cut the tooth and filed it. She looked in the mirror and she was so happy that she started kissing my hand.

During this time, we got a letter from my uncle's son, Nazar, in Aleppo. He had heard from someone that we were alive in Deir el-Zor. We started to communicate with each other. In 1919 we were finally getting ready to leave for Aleppo when we got a second letter telling us not to come. I am guessing that, because of a British ploy, seven to eight hundred Armenians had been massacred in Aleppo.[47]

---

[47] After the start of consolidation of the Nationalist-Kemalist forces in Turkey, a massacre of the Armenians of Aleppo took place on Feb. 28, 1919. The Arabs were instigated by the Turks to attack the Armenians.
Sarkissian, Khacher, *My Memoirs of Seventy Years*. G. Donigian & Fils, Beirut, Lebanon. 1970. P. 828-829.

CHAPTER 4

The British had come to Aleppo by way of Damascus, but they had not entered the city. They had camped around Sebil, under tents. When this massacre and pilfering of the stores had started, the Armenians right away had notified the British that the Arabs were killing them. The British soldiers were having tea at the time and for this reason were late for a few hours in arriving.

Finally when they entered the city with tanks to inquire about the Armenians, it was too late. However, the British never wanted to get involved and did not care about what had happened to the Armenians. Meanwhile we were misled feeling secure that the British were coming to protect us.

Turkish Propaganda Against the Armenians

GM: Was there something in writing from the Turks for Arabs to kill the Armenians?

AK: Yes, in Deir el-Zor I came into possession of a pamphlet published to incite the Arabs against the Armenians. It was a pamphlet of pictures of all the confiscated guns and bombs which they had displayed from each town. The government wanted the native Arabs of the different towns to become our enemies. That way they would not keep us in their homes or help us. Do you understand?

Chapter 5

Aleppo! My father describes coming to the safety of Aleppo at last:

Aleppo with its famous Citadel (1924 postcard cliché by V. Derounian, Alep,Syrie).[48]

We finally arrived in Aleppo in 1919. We walked on Khandek Street where the goldsmith shops were, looking for work. There was a man who was working in Selim Vartan's store; he looked just like the man who had separated from us earlier on that road near the Euphrates River. I approached him and I asked, "Are you Sapsezian," thinking that it might be the same person. "Is your name Kevork?" He said, "No, that's my brother." He interrupted his work and started asking me questions. I told him about all the unfortunate events that had taken place. I said,

---

[48] The Aleppo Citadel is a fortified palace with a surrounding moat from the 3rd millennium B.C. The majority of the construction originates from Ayyubid period following Greek and Byzantine occupation.

CHAPTER 5

"Your brother and three of his four children are dead; only your niece has survived." The man started crying. My father and I started crying with him, too. That's all....

Making a Living

Making a living in Aleppo was difficult in those days. My two uncles carried on with the family trade and started making Sterling silverware, filigree forks and bowls. My father tried his hand at a number of different jobs. These included money changing, arak producing and eventually gas station and automotive lubricant store ownership.

When poor Armenian survivors started to pour into Aleppo, the Protestant Church offered them free flour for making bread, provided they were willing to come to worship in their church. However as the people got established and were able to manage on their own, the church stopped their free flour program. At that point some of the Armenians started attending their longstanding *Lusavorchagan* (Apostolic) Church, Karasoun Mangantz (Forty Martyrs) in the confines of the walled historic city of Aleppo.

When the Protestant minister approached them concerning their lack of attendance at the Protestant Church, they answered, "The flour ended, so did the faith!" (*Un bitti, din bitti*! in Turkish.)

The money changing store in Aleppo was basically a hole in the wall near the main square called *Bab al-Faraj* (Observation Gate of the old walled city). It had a glass case demonstrating a variety of coins and the paper money of different countries. My father also dealt with some small antiquities that were frequently unearthed in and around the city that Arab peasants brought into town for sale. They would find them while tilling the land when their plough would hit something solid. It would turn out to be ancient pottery or clay tablets, which French and English soldiers were interested in buying. Once father had a number of small clay tablets with cuneiform writings that were in great demand, but he did not have an ample supply of these for sale. He decided to reproduce additional ones with small variations of the lettering on limestone, which was readily available in the area. He aged the stones by burying them in the ground and urinating on them! When some of the soldiers returned for additional antiquities, they said they took them to the Museum in London to be assessed. The experts there said that the tablets were old with Hittite letters, but the writings on them did not make any sense.

Extended Kitabjian family has arrived in Aleppo (1920) having survived the Genocide. Patriarch Krikor Kitabjian, seated. To his right is Arous Ana and son Haig and behind him standing, Artin and Parsegh on his right. On his left is Antigone Kitabjian (uncle Garabed's wife) holding grandson Garbis Kitabjian and her daughter Perouz Kitabjian on her left. Standing behind her left to right; her son and spouse Artin G. Kitabjian and Narguiz Kitabjian, her other daughter and son Alice Kitabjian and Nazar Kitabjian. (The couple standing on the left were good friends of my father, name unknown).

CHAPTER 5

Raki, Basterma, and Cats

Before my father decided to run a gas station in Aleppo, he tried to make a living by producing and selling the most popularly consumed liquor in that part of the world, *Raki* (Arak). Pure alcohol was obtained and the percentage was adjusted; then it was mixed with anise extract and bottled. The business was profitable. In his zeal to be helpful, he would lecture to his regular customers against excessive drinking. The men would laugh at him and say that he was hurting his own business. He could not help telling them what he felt was right, although he knew it certainly would not help his income.

When we lived in Aleppo, as a true Gesaratsi, every year my father would make his own *Basterma* (spicy cured meat). He similarly felt that as a Gesaratsi, the ability to make the perfect basterma was a gift that belonged only to them. Making and especially slicing it the right way into very thin slices was a point of pride and honor for him. Initially he would clear the meat, cut it into wide strips and then he would salt them and press them under heavy weights to get all the fluid out. The name *Basterma* means "pressed" in Turkish. Then the meat would hang with strings from a pole to dry, which he would follow by placing it in a bowl full of *chaman*[49] for spicing. Then he would dry it once again.

AK: [In Gesaria] every house used to slaughter a cow once a year. They would make basterma from it and the fat would be melted down, because where we lived was very cold during the winter and would snow. The basterma and Erishik (Armenian sausage), would feed a family for one year. During the summer, nothing would happen to the basterma since it was salted to preserve it. It would

---

[49] Chaman Paste spicing was a combination of paprika, allspice, red pepper, cayenne, cumin, nutmeg, cloves and garlic. It is pasted on the cured meat and again hanged to dry before storage.

not spoil.

* * *

Back in Aleppo, on one occasion my father noticed that while the wide strips of meat were hanging to dry on the balcony of our third story apartment building, one of the pieces had gone missing. He could not imagine how a cat or any other animal could get to them at night. After it happened a second time, the following night he decided to stay awake to catch the culprit. He noticed that a cat jumped from a window with wrought iron bars from the nearby stairway onto the balcony railing, to get to the hanging meat. My father, in his anger, grabbed the cat from its tail and threw it down to the street below. To his amazement, the cat landed on all four feet and ran away down the street.

* * *

Fast forward to Eagle Rock, California in 1957, my father had just emigrated from Syria. Although he was happy to be with the other family members, he still missed his friends and felt distanced from the people and the world he knew; besides he did not know the language and could not drive.

He was well known in Aleppo and well regarded for his common sense, to the point that people would come to his store to ask his opinion on various subjects. While walking down the street, he would frequently meet people who greeted him saying, "Artin Agha." On Sunday afternoons we would go for a walk down Suleymanieh Street. Invariably taxicab drivers would recognize him and stop to offer him a free ride. My father would refuse vehemently, to the displeasure of us kids who wanted to experience riding in a car. We would later ask him why he had refused. He would

CHAPTER 5

say that if he accepted a free service, then they would expect favors from him in the future. Once a gentleman we met while walking asked, "Artin Agha, do you recognize me?" My father answered, "Of course, I know you very, VERY well." Later he said to us, "Do you know why I answered him that way? It is because he owes me money from the past and he thought I had forgotten him."

Since he was lonely and depressed and wanted to be useful, he started working at the rug cleaning plant on Riverside Drive in the Atwater Village section of Los Angeles owned by my two maternal uncles. In addition, he decided to make *Basterma* to sell for profit. One Saturday we drove south on Atlantic Boulevard to the Rosemead-Montebello area to get some fillet cuts of meat from an Armenian butcher. My father got all the fat and sinews out and fixed the *Basterma* with great care. He was especially careful for it not to show any fat upon slicing. We took his finished product back to the butcher for it to be weighed. "You cannot make any money at this rate," he said, "besides you have to charge so much more to recover your cost, let alone your labor." We took the *Basterma* home to eat it ourselves.

Every month he would go to the Central Market on Spring Street in Los Angeles to buy a leg of lamb. He would bring it home and cut it and clean out the fat and sinews so it could be used for kebab. He would grind part of it with a manual grinder, divide and label it into a number of packages, which he froze for later use. He would also freeze the fat until it was garbage pickup day, so it would not spoil and smell in the garbage can. Before the garbage-collector arrived, he would take it out of the freezer and put it on top of the garbage can. When the Afro-American garbage-collector initially noticed that it was fat cuttings, he put it in his cab for his personal use. Eventually father developed a good relationship with the garbage-collector and they communicated without words; he would wait and hand him the frozen fat cuttings wrapped in aluminum foil and in return, the garbage-collector would be kind to his metal garbage cans; he would not bang them hard or allow them to roll down the steep hill on Wawona Street.

Return to Gesaria: Father describes his return to Gesaria in 1919 soon after arriving in Aleppo:

> *At that time, I travelled from Giligia (Cilicia) through Bozanti and I went to Gesaria. A few of our surviving friends had also returned. My main concern was that I had hidden gold, silver, old antiques, as well as money in the walls of our home. I can say that my father and his two brothers were first class jewelers, goldsmiths and silversmiths. We hid these items in Gesaria, because we couldn't take them with us.*

The Hidden Gold:

> *When I got there, I found out that some Turks were living in our house. I appealed to the Government to receive the key for our house. Within three days they gave us the key. I entered the house. The walls where I had hidden all these valuables were torn down; that meant that everything was gone. My last hope disappeared into thin air.*

Worthless Lead Bars

Father also checked the animal barn. Under the donkey excrement, he found two bars of worthless lead he had hidden right before leaving Gesaria.

He went to the barbershop for a haircut with the intention of picking up any gossip he may come across. The barber recognized him right away. "Aren't you Kirkor's son? What are you doing here? If they find you here, they will kill you. Take the next train back to Haleb." Mustafa Kemal's forces were sweeping down from Eastern Anatolia and cleansing all of Turkey of other nationalities, including Greeks and the few remaining Armenians who had survived the genocide and had returned back to what they considered to be their true homeland.

Here is the part from his interview concerning this risky trip:

GM: Did you go back to Gesaria?

AK: I went to Gesaria in mid-1919. We had hidden a large amount of gold and antiques... I hid these in the middle of the walls with my own hands, since there were empty spaces there, but I may have made mistakes. I went back to claim those things so we could have some ready money, but I did not succeed. Instead, I ended up spending an additional 25 gold pieces and I came back empty-handed.

GM: You went to Gesaria to find those things and came back to Aleppo and stayed until 1956?

AK: Yes. It was 1919; Mustafa Kemal was coming to Sivas. In Gesaria a famous government person knew me; I wanted to know from him what the political situation was. He asked me whether I came to stay or would be leaving. It was the June of 1919. I told him I had some work to do, that's why I came. That man told me to leave as soon as possible, since in five days it was their holy day (Ramazan) and on the last day of the feast, they would collect men for the draft. "No one will be able to save you since you are a Turkish citizen," he said. I had shown him my identification card (*Nufus kaghidi*) to get the keys to our homes.

GM: The French?

AK: No, the Turks. There were no French forces there. We had two homes and the store. I was checking on the things we had hidden. Because the walls of our homes were made of stone and in between there were small pieces to keep the stones straight. When I went to the basement, I saw that those small stones had fallen to the floor. After we had left Gesaria, they had rented the homes and the occupants had pushed metal rods; when they had heard the sound of metal, they had taken out all the hidden valuables.

Killing of Grandmother's Children

AK: …. My grandmother had stayed in Gesaria; her family was able to stay there because they were Armenian Catholics. When my Grandfather died at a young age, she remarried and had two children. Those two children were thrown into a gorge in Talas[50]. They had collected 800 children between ages 8 and 15 and all of them were thrown there and killed.
GM: What year was this?
AK: This was in 1916. They were my uncles. I was told this by my Grandmother.
GM: Didn't they adopt the young ones?
AK: No. They wanted to kill them. They would adopt only 1-2 year olds.
GM: Below the age of 5.
AK: They did not want to adopt the older ones since they could not convert them; they knew too much. It must have been hard.
GM: Once you learn the Armenian language, it was too late to be converted.
AK: Yes. That is right.

Traitors:

> *When I went to Gesaria, I asked about the traitor, Mihran Yazejian, "That man, where is he now?" There were no Armenians left therefore there was no need for him. He with his family had gone to Istanbul. "That is a big city," he said to himself, "We can hide there and I will survive." There were Armenians who pursued him. One day they entered his apartment and tied him up, including his three*

---

[50] "Zinci Dere" which was located outside the city in a desolate region. There was another valley called "Derevank" closer to the Armenian Missionary School. Stephen Zurnacian, personal communication.

children and his wife. They killed them all. First the three children, the wife and afterwards, Mihran.

The people in the apartment below complained to the government officials of a bad smell coming from the upstairs unit. They went to the apartment; they broke the door. What they saw was an entire family lined up and killed. I wish I could kiss the hands of the people who killed them.[51]

<u>Massacre of Returnees</u>: My father speaks:

Massacres, deportation and war ended. We returned to Aleppo, but I was thinking about returning to Giligia (Cilicia) because the liars, the French, had promised that Giligia was going to be returned to the Armenians. Liars. They signed a treaty with the Turks[52] *and afterwards they surrendered Giligia to the Turks. Returnees to Hadjin and Marash were massacred again. Aintab and Izmir had great losses. Because the great powers, England, France and Italy had come to an understanding with the Turks. The Turks proceeded in massacring half of the Armenians who had previously escaped their wrath. The European governments were gone and had left us defenseless. We*

---

[51] Besides Yazudjian there were other traitors and identifiers.
1. Minas Minassian was one of the first traitors. After his usefulness had come to an end he was hanged with his victims.
2. Hovagim Yezekielian, caretaker of St. Lusavorich church, blamed Archpriest Gemitchian, for the cache of guns in the church and that he was forced to hide them. Still, for this reason he was also hanged.
3. Kevork Yelanjian, traitor of Tashnak Party members.
From Alboyajian, pp. 1410-1412.

[52] Treaty of Lausanne, July 24, 1923 which returned a lot of the territory that had been taken away from Turkish control by the Treaty of Sevres in 1920 at the end of WWI.

were thinking and applauding that these Christian governments were coming to help us. Alas! It did not turn out to be that way. If the power is not in your hands, you cannot defend your rights.

<u>Protestation to the Creator of This World</u>: My father speaks to God and God answers!

*They say that there must be a creator.
To be living in this world is a miracle,
It is truly a paradise,
People come and go with that belief.
It is too complicated for people to comprehend.
Until now no one has understood your creations.*

*Where are you, Creator!
After having finished your work, are you watching from the sidelines?
From the days of my life's long travels of eighty years,
I was unable to tolerate all the tortures that the Armenian nation was subjected to.
Are we responsible because we cannot get along with other nations?
We believe that you would treat all of your children equally,
No matter what religion they belong to.*

*I am amazed to watch what cruelty is carried out by ruthless and evil nations,
And they go unpunished.*

*If there is a God, why does he allow these things to happen?
It is enough, God, this is not a life.*

CHAPTER 5

Why did you create us to witness these days of suffering?
Our forefathers worked with love so that we also could enjoy this paradise.
Why this much inequality?
You know that we are made of flesh and blood and not like bronze statues,
That we could remain unaffected by so many difficulties
A father or a creator would not settle for so much favoritism.
That means there is no justice.

Instead, your anger touches us directly.
1895, one year before I was born,
300 thousand Armenians were massacred in Turkey.
And in the Adana Massacre of 1909, 30 thousand were killed.
During the Great Massacre of 1915, I was in it, one and half million perished.
Did you see what the cruel Turks did to us all the way to Deir el-Zor?
I was in it and witnessed it with others of our countrymen; I said, "There is no God."
It seems you were too busy with the War and forgot about us, the Armenians.

The invasion of Cyprus where the civilized U.S. helped the Turks,
It did a lot of harm to Greeks and Armenians.
Now, coming to the Lebanon war,
The previous Christian and Muslim nations had issues to settle.
They wanted to eliminate the Christian government.

LEAVING KAYSERI

The major nations, U.S. and Russia, they allowed Lebanese to kill each other.
For 15 months no one said, "Come, let us see what the problem is?"
During this misery, 250 thousand Armenians were hungry and thirsty,
Running all here and there, not knowing where to escape.
Meanwhile, you were watching.
Well, you made the Turks happy!

Apparently, the law of the land favors the evil.
If we had nothing good to accomplish,
If we were a hated nation, and not dear to your heart,
You might as well annihilate us.
Then your beneficent heart could rest.
As you know, we are a peace loving people.
The nations who profess peace are liars,
And do not see the damage being done to other nations.

They work for their own benefit.
During all these years the Armenian people lived a hellish dream.

The Turks were after annihilating a constructive nation.
They always used to tell us that we were one hundred years ahead of them,
And for us to wait so they could catch up with us.
It has been 80 years and they are at the same place,
While we have advanced,
Except for the loss of 1.5 million
Plus the additional generations that would have been born.
And now we have been scattered all over the world.

CHAPTER 5

Now after numerous sufferings, we have an Armenia.
We are thankful that we have come to our senses.
As a nation we see ourselves to be superior, in spite of our small numbers.
If we had come to an understanding with our powerful neighbors,
We would have been better off.
We do not live and thrive well among thorns.
The fault is ours.
We approached the wrong sources, to nations without pity.
We did not know how to deal with our neighbors.

Now that I have reached this old age
When I hear the name Deir el-Zor,
My whole body shakes,
It is impossible to forget.
Only death will make one forget.
No matter how much I write, my heart will not be contented.
Only and only those who passed through those roads
Know what the Armenian nation suffered in the hands of the cruel Turks,
And it is hard to explain to others who have not experienced it.
Creator! Pity the Armenian Nation.
The Armenian nation is only a dot on this sphere;
Pity them since what they have suffered in the hands of cruel nations is enough,
They promise but do not deliver on their promises.
You have given control of this paradise
To seven or eight cruel and pitiless powerful nations

LEAVING KAYSERI

They make it hell for the majority of the people
While they derive enjoyment.
Creator, since you are the master of this Universe,
Why do you allow these cruel nations to divide amongst them your inheritance?

This paradise does not have heirs, is infinite, and has absolutely no end.

Creator, those who came before, have told the newcomers that there is a creator,
And on that premise we have come to enjoy the paradise
But no one has met your major powers.
Similarly, I have not been worthy of any of your miracles.

They say that there is a Creator,
People come and go by saying and believing that.

(God answers)
   "Quiet! Quiet! Traveler!
   I heard what you are saying;
   This world is a miraculous paradise.
   All those who come are amazed,
   At the same time this world is a mystery.
   The ones that are born think that it belongs to them.
   But it is a mistake.
   When the final day arrives, you will leave all and go.
   This paradise is for the ones that can enjoy it.
   If you have brains use it and enjoy it.
   Do not look for another paradise, because there is none.
   It will be hell for those who do not know its value".

Artin Kitabjian

CHAPTER 5

They Come and Go

My father's favorite poem by Ashugh Chivan, a traveling minstrel.

  (Translated by Gregory Ketabgian)

  Wretched days, like winter
  They come and go.
  Not to be discouraged, they end,
  They come and go.
  Intense pains do not remain
  Long on people.
  Like a line of customers
  They come and go.

  Peril, pursuit and trouble
  On top of nations
  Like travelling caravans
  They come and go.
  The world is a special garden
  And people, flowers.
  How many violets, roses, balsam
  Come and go?

  Neither let the powerful gloat
  Nor the weak be sad.
  Varied, changeable people
  They come and go.
  Without fear the sun
  Projects its light,
  The clouds towards the temple
  Come and go.

  The world is caressing the educated child.
  Like a mother,

LEAVING KAYSERI

Vulgar, nomadic races
Come and go.
The world is a hospice, Chivan!
People are visitors,
This is the natural order.
They come and go.

Enameled Silver Snuffbox left from Kayseri.

CHAPTER 5

Chapter 6

Meeting Mother

From his business in Aleppo, everyday my father would notice four sisters[53] walking across the street. He specially felt attracted to the youngest one that had a fair complexion. He asked his brother Parsegh to follow the sisters to find out where they lived. Through a mutual acquaintance, they eventually met the parents for a marriage proposal. This left Yacoub and Mariam Matossians, my mother's parents, in a quandary. According to custom, the youngest daughter would not be allowed to marry until the older three sisters were spoken for.

As my mother would relate it, my grandfather had said to my grandmother, "Mariam, we will have one less mouth to feed, let her get married." The Matossians had recently arrived in Aleppo from Aintab. The girls were the sole breadwinners of the family doing needlework. In this way they were helping to send their three younger brothers to school. My grandfather had worked in Aintab as the recorder of deeds and was unable to find employment in a foreign country such as Syria. Customs and foods varied quite a bit between Gesaria and Aintab. Gesaratsis felt that they were more refined and had taken on more European customs than Aintabtsis. Aintabtsis were more relaxed and fun loving people. Gesaratsis had to be offered something three times and decline it, before they would finally accept it. This way they thought they would look more civilized! After they were engaged, when my father was a guest for dinner at the Matossian household for the first time, he almost went home hungry since each time he was offered a dish, he would say, "No thank you" and they would pass him up, instead of offering it again.

---

[53] Their oldest sister, Behia, had come to the U.S. as a picture bride in 1920 and had married Mihran Tejirian in Chicago.

CHAPTER 6

The types of food were also quite different. Aintabtsi dishes included *dolmas, sarmas* and *kufta* varieties, while my father was more familiar with *manti, beoreg,* and *kata.*

Marriage and Children:

Wedding Portrait, September 21, 1925 in Aleppo, Syria.

In 1925, I got married to Beatrice, the daughter of Yacoub and Mariam Matossian. We were blessed with three children, Arpiné, Shaké, and Krikor.

The Broken Window

"It's enough," My mother was pleading with my father who was beating the soles of my feet with a piece of firewood, after he had come home in the evening and found out that I had broken the plate glass of the dining room door. "I want him to know how hard it is to earn money during the war," was what I heard my father shout over my wails.

It was during World War II that among other manufactured goods, there was a shortage of glass. Before the war began, my father had stockpiled many foodstuffs and other necessary items such as wheat, bulgur, fat, sugar and *bekmez* (molasses), as well as soap, which was stored under my bed. I had to smell the soap constantly if I was sleeping on that side of the bed.

My sister Shaké and I would get into fights. I remember running after her with a heavy broom in my outstretched hand as she ran into the dining room and closed the door quickly. In my anger, I could not stop the downward movement of the broom. It came down hard on the glass of the door, smashing it into pieces.

It was my father's cautious philosophy that had saved him and his family members from a certain death during the march through the Syrian Desert. The facts were, as he saw it: **that the future was unknown, governments could not be trusted, one should be self-reliant and that one should be prepared for the worst-case scenario**. I would call this a survivor's philosophy. It seemed somewhat pessimistic at the time but it prepared one for survival. I am sure his realism had developed as a result of his previous painful experiences; but it was not a defeatist philosophy. It encouraged one to work harder to succeed and to prepare for the future. However, this philosophy sometimes got in the way of planning for vacations and celebrating happy occasions, since each time my mother would ask him to make plans for a summer vacation, he would say, "Let's see if we are still alive by then."

As World War II dragged on, sugar and flour shortages developed. The government had instituted food rationing for flour and sugar and would hand out a limited number of coupons (*bon*) for each family. People had to go and wait in line to get their supplies. Since we had adequate supplies, my mother would give the coupons to my aunts.

CHAPTER 6

My mother would get wheat grinders who would bring a heavy grinding machine with two large wheels with handles, up the apartment stairs. They would grind the wheat into bulgur (cracked wheat) or into fine flour. But before the wheat was ground up, my mother and her sisters would sit around a wide tray and separate the wheat from pieces of stone and gravel that had mixed in during the separation of the wheat from the shaft by the peasants. My mother would distribute some of it to my aunts who had more modest financial resources.

* * *

The only close encounter we had with the war was when the British Air Force decided to bomb the railroad yards in Aleppo. These were not too far from our house. The reason this was done was mainly to prevent the German forces from getting the oil out of Baghdad to the Mediterranean theatre. At that time Syria was under the Vichy French rule which sided with the Germans. The air raids were preannounced by the local French regime and we were advised to blacken our windows and turn off all the lights. We were also advised to go to the basement when the sirens blared. Being curious, my father would wait until the last second to do so. He and I would be outside in front of our apartment building waiting for the plane to show up. We watched as a single engine plane with a sputtering-sounding motor came directly towards us from the east. We ran down the stairs to the basement which was full of Muslim women from the other floors of the building. Besides the sound of the bombs exploding and shaking the ground, the only other excitement was my sister Shaké, who was born with a weak stomach. She would start retching and vomiting. This caused great alarm among the Muslim women from the second floor who came to help my mother to care for her.

LEAVING KAYSERI

After the "all clear" signal was given, we all ran to the roof to see what had happened. We could see some flames coming from the railroad yards from the south. The bombing and subsequent fire destroyed my cousin Hrair's father's delicatessen at the railroad station. Once I found some shrapnel on our side balcony, which I kept for a long time as a souvenir of the war.

In 1940, my father had gotten one of the first Phillips shortwave radios in Aleppo.[54] Every evening he would listen to the news from BBC in Turkish, as well as from Cairo, Egypt. During the war it was illegal to own a shortwave radio. He had draped a long needlework over it, to make it less obvious. He would keep his hand on the dial to adjust for the static called *"parasit"* which would at times make the news inaudible. On occasion, during the critical phases of the war, friends and neighbors would come to listen to the progress of the Allies.[55]

My father also had gotten a glossy map of Europe, which he had mounted on the wall. On it he would follow the troop movements with the small flags of each country involved. Without being aware of it, the map had become an educational tool for us cousins. We spent countless hours playing "find the capital" games. My favorite winning capital was Reykjavik, as it was difficult to find Iceland in the Northern Atlantic.

* * *

Sometime during the war, my father had applied for an immigration visa for our family to emigrate to the U.S., knowing that this would be a long process and would probably take years for our name to come up on

---

[54] In 1936 he had a Pilot shortwave radio.
[55] Once he had invited some friends and relatives to come and listen to the broadcast of Soorp Znoont Mass broadcast from Jerusalem. As the program had progressed, the people present were amazed that they even could smell *khoong* (incense) from the broadcast. Unnoticed by them, my father had put a small amount of incense on the stove which permeated the aroma through the room. This piece of memory is supplied by my sister Shaké Balekjian.

CHAPTER 6

their long list. At that time immigration into the U.S. was run on a quota system, meaning that each country was allowed a limited number of immigrants to enter the U. S. per year. This number was determined according to the percentage of the people residing in the U.S. of that country at the time the law was passed (1921). It was mainly a way of limiting immigrants from Asian countries, mainly the Chinese, since the majority of the population of the United States at that time was composed of English, Irish, German, Italian and other Europeans. The total number of quotas per year allotted for countries like Syria and Turkey was 100 as a gesture of good will.

My father had completely forgotten about this application until one day a letter arrived from the U.S. Embassy. Members of our entire family were being asked to have physical examinations, chest x-rays, blood, urine, and stool tests and then come in for a visa application. This presented a dilemma for all of us, since we were not yet mentally prepared for a move out of Syria; however we all went ahead with the evaluation. Everything went well except for my father's stool tests, which repeatedly came back positive for parasites, in spite of repeated treatments for worms by his physician. It was common to have roundworm (Ascaris lumbricoidis) infestation in Aleppo, due to poor sanitation and the use of night soil in vegetable farming. After the third attempt, my father became frustrated and asked me to give my stool sample to use instead of his specimen.

After all that preparation, the U.S. Embassy said that the visa was only for my older sister, Arpiné. Since she did not wish to travel alone and be separated from the family, she forfeited her right to the quota. This brought an avalanche of young Armenian men who wanted her to give them her number. This of course was a false impression on their part, since it was not up to her to give it away. The following year her quota number came up again; by then my sister was ready to take the plunge. My sister Shaké and I followed her after three years. However, my parents had to wait until my sister Arpiné had become a U.S. citizen, to be able to request for their immigration visas. Otherwise due to being born in Turkey, their quota number would have never come up in Syria.

The Arab Landlord

We lived on the top floor of a three story apartment building we rented in Aleppo from a Muslim Arab lawyer, who had an eccentric personality. He would talk by bending down to the floor and motioning with his hands while constantly looking at the floor, as if he was an actor in a Greek tragedy.

The building was above a public water fountain (*Ayn-Tel*) on Suleymanieh Street, where horse drawn carriages used to come to water the horses as well as to rest them in the shadow of the apartment building during the hot and dry summer afternoons. People who lived in the poorer sections of town, a few blocks to the east, came there to get their water and carried it in pails to their homes.

To the north of us was an area of empty land which we called the *Anabad* (Desert), where some of the original Armenian refugees having survived the massacres in the Syrian Desert, had settled and built a shanty town. Since then it had been demolished; but when we sometimes took a shortcut to my cousin Zaven's house through this area, we could still see the imprints of the old shacks.

Compared to what existed then, we had a fairly advanced bathroom with a regular sit down-toilet and a flush tank close to the ceiling with a hanging chain handle to flush with. It also had a wood-burning water heater, a cold water shower and a low sink for bathing. It had a travertine floor with a drain in one corner. Most of the older homes had no bathing facilities because the old custom was to go to the public baths. The previous home we lived in on Tilel section of town was an older house with a community

CHAPTER 6

toilet. The toilet consisted of two stones with a hole in the center over which you had to squat; it had no running water. To make sure the stool went down to the sewer, one had to nudge and beat it into the hole with a stick that had a well-worn handle polished with repeated use. It looked like an oversized baseball bat. To wash up, we had to go to the kitchen sink. There was only one toilet to be used by two or three families that lived in separate rooms around the courtyard.

I remember when we lived in the Tilel section of town, my mother used to take me to a public bath once a week when we would meet there with my aunts and cousins. I only remember the musty smell of the bath, the echoing sounds and greasy floors. I do not think I was sexually aware at that time, but the chief lady in charge at the door once told my mother that I had matured and had added, "Why don't you bring his father with him next time."

After moving to the apartment in Suleymanieh, Saturdays were designated to be the bath days in our home. Mother would warm up the water by building a wood fire under the tank and we would take turns taking a bath. My aunts would also come to take their baths in the afternoon and stay for a light supper, which was mainly tea, olives and cheese with some pastries, usually *kaghge* or *kata*. It gave us the three cousins time to clown around and play games. I had become famous for marching in a goosestep and putting olives in my tea.

My father had decided that the bathroom needed a small window for ventilation and lighting. He had a mason come to make an opening to install a window about eight by twelve inches. Somehow the landlord found out about it and sued my father for damages, in addition to raising the rental fee. It was a serious matter for an Armenian to be sued by a Muslim lawyer, since the judges were all Muslim and were expected to side with their own kind. We were all afraid and anxious. My father hired a Muslim attorney recommended by his Muslim clients. We won the case because of the poor reputation of our landlord. In addition, the landlord was fined for not having a window in a bathroom which was required according to the building code. Additionally, he was ordered to lower our rent for the next six months.

My father had a lot of Arab landowners as his clients. They used to grow wheat and cotton further east from Aleppo and needed gas for their trucks. His gas station was conveniently located outside the city borders on the northeastern part of town. All the other gas stations were owned by Arabs. They trusted my father for unadulterated gas and he honored their credit, since they had to take the wheat or cotton to market for sale before they could pay for their expenses. Most of the truck drivers were Armenian with good knowledge of the workings of the truck engines. At times they would be stuck on the highway with a broken axle due to overloading and needed spare parts to be sent to them for repairs.

My father's relationship with the wealthy Arab landowners would come in handy repeatedly when governmental or legal problems arose. During Israel's independence in 1947 and during the first Arab-Israeli War, Jewish businesses and stores were all plundered and then put to the torch.[56] I remember one Sunday afternoon when we got up on our roof and could see black smoke rising from the central part of town.

A Jewish businessman, a colleague of my uncle Parsegh, happened to knock on their door during the 1st Arab-Israeli War one evening and asked them to hide him until he could get a false passport to leave the country. They took him in and eventually he left in three days. Subsequently police came looking for him. But not finding him, they searched the house and found a handgun in the linen closet. It was illegal to own a handgun in Syria. They arrested my uncle and took him to the central jail. My aunt Knarig asked me to run as fast as I could to my father's store to tell him

---

[56] Aleppo Pogrom of 1947.

what had happened. She wanted my father to try to get him out of jail. The typical procedure after one was jailed in Syria was to give him an intense beating before any interrogation took place. Thus speed was an important factor in this case. Through my father's contacts, my uncle was soon released before any beating had taken place. He later had to pay a fine.

I knew my father had a rifle hidden in our home, but as a child I was unable to find its location. My sister Shaké knew it to be a German Mauser which was hidden in a false compartment on top of the armoire in my parents' bedroom.

My Maternal Aunt Vahidé

My aunt Vahidé's family lived on top of a narrow cobblestone street lined with stores, mainly jewelers, barbers and other Armenian artisans. Further down the street, one would see a huge iron gate with nails on it that opened to a fairly large courtyard which enclosed the old historic Karasoon Mangantz and Soorp Astvazazin Armenian Churches as well as a Greek Orthodox Church. This was a remnant from the old walled city; of course the gate did not close now, but remained as a reminder of how the churches in the old days had to be protected against attacks from the outside.

The house they lived in was also one of the old, historic Arab homes with a courtyard that had a nonfunctional fountain in the center. It consisted of a number of large rooms all surrounding the courtyard and each occupied by an Armenian family. My aunt's family occupied the only upstairs room with the adjoining kitchen and toilet area. Next to it was an extensive flat roof which was used by all the families to sleep on during the hot summer nights of Aleppo. It was a beautiful experience to fall asleep while looking at the starlit dark sky before all the present light pollution obliterated it.

The large room occupied by the family was divided into two

sections by a brown bureau and a separating screen. The area with the windows and an overhang was the living room, while the other section served as my aunt's workplace where she did her seamstress work. There was a waist high closet in the passageway that was taken up by my cousin Hrair's collection of odds and ends that we would use to "fix" all the necessary items for our experiments.

As far as I could remember, most of the time my Aunt Vahidé was the main breadwinner, since her husband, Hrant Dekmejian, was ill. He was unable to run the delicatessen at the railroad station after it was damaged due to the bombing of the railroad yards by the British during the Second World War. He would sit by the corner of the couch near the window and read. From time to time he would ask for warm milk to sooth his painful stomach. He was born into an Armenian family that had immigrated to Aleppo from Erzurum a few generations before the massacres. They were in the brass casting business, thus the last name *Deukmeji*, which refers to pouring molten brass into forms. He was well educated and had a solid knowledge of the Arabic language. He also had a number of intellectual friends. Once I had the chance to meet a friend of his who had been active in fighting against the Turks and had lost his vision and some of his fingers, when a bomb he was constructing exploded.

My aunt was a capable dressmaker. Her clients would bring a picture from a magazine and the material to be sewn and she would come up with a similar outfit, but it would involve a number of *"prova"*s (fitting sessions). These would become more like a social gathering of clients, friends and family members and of course would include a course of Armenian coffee after it was hand-ground by one of the people present. The coffee sessions would not be complete without my aunt reading their fortunes from the down-turned cups, a talent in which she excelled among many others.

* * *

CHAPTER 6

Into this setting came my cousin Hrair, who would jump in with a request for money to buy a necessary item for an experiment or project, followed by myself and our other cousin Zaven. In spite of their financial situation, my aunt would never turn him down.

She was committed to providing him with all the necessary experiences and education. She worked hard to be able to give her children the best education available. This also included violin lessons for Hrair and piano lessons for her daughter Mary.

Having noticed these events taking place often at their home, my sister Shaké had written an essay in high school about a poor family who did not skimp on their son's need for a magnet to be used in an experiment to build a compass. The article was entered in a writing contest by the teacher and later chosen to be published in a school publication. Having read the article, my aunt's family had felt upset after recognizing the resemblance. They felt bad for being thought of as being poor.

Hrair's request at one of these times was for five piasters (cents) to buy a Ping-Pong ball. He had gotten two old wooden door panels from the wrecked remnants of the railroad station after the bombing, for a ping pong table, some cheese cloth for the netting and had built rackets from plywood, having glued sandpaper on the paddles. We had learned the fundamentals of playing ping pong that summer, but had to be careful to avoid the holes on the doors where the door handle had been, as well as other irregularities on the wood that would send the ball in acute but challenging angles. The games sometimes came to an abrupt end when the neighbors who occupied the rooms downstairs complained about the dust that came raining down on their furniture from the ceiling.

One summer Hrair had found a lab workbook from some abandoned papers from the Aleppo College Library and had decided to perform every experiment in it. That summer we built a crystal radio, wrapped an armature to generate electricity and built electric motors. We also built a compass and poured molten lead into molds carved out of limestone. Hrair got most of his supplies free from his neighbors like Baron Puzant and Garabed Yegavian, electrical contractors where Hrair worked during summers. Some of these neighbors were into reconditioning old electric motors, batteries, and car engines. Actually, a lot of reconditioning and rebuilding went on by many Armenian mechanics and tool and die makers, because spare parts were either not available or very expensive in Aleppo at the time. Hrair's endless energy and insatiable appetite for knowledge and discovery was infectious and would rub off on me and Zaven. We looked forward to go to their home to visit, to see what he had come up with for us to experience that day.

Bed Bugs and Aleppo Boils

It was hard to find where the bed bugs would hide during the day, since our bed frames had numerous steel springs and hollow metal legs. They would only surface at night and come to suck our blood and leave. We would wake up with intense itching bites and rarely see a bug crawling away fully engorged with its victim's blood. It was not a good idea to smash the culprit, although one would be tempted to do so. Besides staining the bed sheets, it would release an awful smell, probably due to old digested blood.

It seemed like the bugs were travelling from one bed to another. This frustrated my father. He would be very good at winning the battles against bugs due to his experience with lice and typhus during the deportation. He would be ready with his hand-pumped sprayer full of DDT and kerosene that used to have crystallized DDT on its cover, but it seemed that the sprayed DDT did not penetrate inside the tubing of the bed frames. Eventually the solution was found by putting the legs of the beds into cans filled with a DDT-kerosene mixture. The bugs were either killed or ran away from the constant smell of the kerosene in our bedrooms!

CHAPTER 6

My father also made sure that our living quarters were sprayed repeatedly during the summer months, when we would leave home for a trip or excursion.

We were fortunate not to have been bitten by the sand fly that transmitted the Aleppo Boil parasite (Cutaneous Leishmaniasis) that used to be endemic in the area. Most of my classmates had the boil usually on their face that would last for months and was very difficult to cure. It would eventually leave a very prominent scar.

They would treat it with a purple-white cream that probably had gentian violet and zinc oxide in it, but seemed it was not very effective. It appeared that the students who lived in *"Nor Kugh"* (New Village) part of town were more likely to be bitten. This district was mainly inhabited by Armenian Genocide survivors and their families. It mainly consisted of modest homes that were further south, past the Armenian Cemetery. Most knowledgeable people, when I told them that I grew up in Aleppo, would check my face to see where my Aleppo Boil scar was. I am sure the flies were breeding in the dirty waters of the Quayk River behind our house that looked more like a sewer outflow rather than a river. It ran south from Antep but the Turks had cut off the flow of the water at the border. Aintabtsis, according to my mother, had a saying that "Antep peed and Aleppo drank."

My parents were quite protective of all their children and did not wish us to be exposed to any infections or other dangers outside of our home environment. My father would warn me to stay away from some of my friends that looked pale and skinny, due to the fear that they may have tuberculosis. In spite of all the precautions, we still had our share of serious illnesses in addition to the usual childhood diseases. My sister Shaké had typhoid fever which was treated with complete bed rest and clear liquids for one month. One summer we all came down with Dengue Fever, which was quite debilitating.

My father would also not allow me to go down to the street to play with other kids or go out to play soccer with my friends, which prevented me from learning vernacular Arabic. I had a soccer ball with which I used to practice carefully on the flat roof that had only a one meter tall wall around it. One day I kicked it harder than usual and it went over the wall and fell down to the street. As I looked down, I saw a boy pick it up and run away with it. I hurried down the stairs as fast as I could, but there was no trace of the boy or my soccer ball when I got down.

The Old Arab Farmer

Wooden pail coming up from the well
Attached to a green algae covered rope
Knotted, rusted handles and braces
Scraped against the ages old walls.

Youngsters positioning
To be the first ones to quench
Their overwhelming thirst
To consume from the cool
Life giving fluid.

Having seen it all
Old Arab farmer with kind eyes
Knowing full well that
These are children of orphans.

Hot Aleppo sun beating down on us
Among the hills covered with
Black moss covered rocks
Among dark red earth.

Having jostled closer at last
Noted that the water
At the bottom of the pail
Among gravel having wiggling
Worms of green color.

CHAPTER 6

> Drink! Drink! Quickly
> Quench that thirst
> Left from generations past.
> Thirst of curiosity,
> Education foremost. [57]

The Village

The Matossian family of Antep was a landowner before the deportations. They apparently owned close to fifty villages in the surrounding area. When the border between Syria and Turkey was drawn after World War I, two of the villages happened to be situated on the Syrian side.[58] After the deportation from Antep, my grandfather lived in Jarablus, a small town on the Turkish-Syrian border which was close to the villages, where he could supervise the Arab peasants thus additionally providing a partial income for the family. He apparently also worked for Regis Tobacco Company, since he knew the Arabic alphabet. During the ensuing years after the family moved to Beirut for the education of the boys, the land was taken over by Arab settlers. However after some lengthy legal work and investigation by Aunt Vahidé and her husband, as well as financial support by my father, the title of the villages were converted back to the eight descendants of our grandfather, Yacoub Matossian.

Aunt Vahidé, with the support of her husband, took charge of managing the day to day activities of the village. It was run essentially along the lines of a feudal system. The Arab villagers living on the land would survive by sowing the wheat grain supplied by the landowner. They waited for the rain, then they

---

[57] A scene during an elementary school field trip outside the city borders of Aleppo.

[58] The villages were Tel-Shair and Heomur in Jarablus section. They consisted of a total of 165 hectares (60 acres).

harvested it and threshed it manually. The wheat was divided into three portions. One third was for the peasants' use, the second was allocated for seed for the next year and the last third belonged to the landowner to sell. However, it was difficult to hold the peasants to their word. Each year they would ask for additional seed; claiming that the last year's harvest was poor for myriad reasons, including drought, locusts, and so on.

We used to go at times with my aunt to visit the villages. It was a patch of dry reddish dirt. The Arab kids would race after our car and crowd around us, as if they had not seen a white man in those parts of the country for ages. The children would have sun damaged skin, swollen abdomens probably due to protein malnutrition, as well as numerous flies in the corner of their eyes, which they would not bat away. We would be tempted to bat their flies away ourselves. This scene was similar to what one sees in old movies of Africa.

Each time we visited, the villagers would slaughter a lamb, stuff it with rice and cook it over the fire. All the men, as well as aunt Vahidé would sit on the dirt floor of the mud huts they lived in. We all ate with our hands and made small talk. The village women stood behind the men until they were finished.

On one occasion they brought a beautiful Arabian horse for me to ride. I had never been on a horse before in my life. But before I could say anything, I was hoisted upon the bare back of the horse as it took off up a hill on a fairly rapid gallop. I was holding on for dear life on the horse's mane to keep from falling off.

Fortunately, the horse decided to stop when it reached the top of the hill and turned back to look where it had come from. The Arab peasants ran towards me cheering, thinking that I was an accomplished rider!

After everyone in our extended Matossian clan had immigrated to the United States, there was no one to look after the village. The family attempted to donate the village to AGBU. The legal process and paperwork was started in 1971. But trying to prove the legal citizenship of all the heirs to the property turned out to be quite a time consuming process. In between, there was a lapse due to the illness of my father and some of the other members of the family. The correspondence was mainly being carried on by my father with input from Uncle Nerses and the AGBU personnel in New York and then being transmitted and translated to the people in Syria. By the time all the paperwork and deeds were transferred to AGBU, it was found that the land had again been occupied by Arab settlers and AGBU needed to go to court to prove their ownership. As far as we know, that avenue was not pursued. From what I surmise, AGBU was also reluctant to accept it, possibly considering it a difficult asset to dispose of.[59] There was also desire on my uncle Nerses's part to claim it as a tax deduction in the U. S., which made the process much more complicated.

---

[59] AGBU: Armenian General Benevolent Union. Syrian government had become socialist at that time and there was talk of giving peasants land ownership.

Chapter 7

My Mother

Mother

You came and went gently.

Pointing up to heaven
Aphasia blocking your words
Well understood by all.

You wanted to leave
Near the end
Having seen enough injustice
For one human to bear.

My earliest recollection of my mother was that she fell ill frequently while I was in kindergarten. She had to travel to Beirut to be evaluated at the American University of Beirut. Her frequent absences had affected me during my early years of schooling when I was anxious due to not having the maternal support I needed at home. Once I was blamed by my classmates for having broken a window pane. It had actually broken when I was pushed against it by a group of students, but the teacher would not listen to my explanation. My mother's illness must have also affected me emotionally since I might have thought I had caused it, as I had confided to my Aunt Arous. She was fond of repeatedly reminding me about this fact, later on in life. This affected my performance at school and it was decided that I should repeat the year in Kindergarten. Although my Aunt Knarig was available to assist me, it still did not feel the same as maternal support.

CHAPTER 7

It was not clear what illness my mother had. It seemed like an ill-defined leg pain accompanied by abdominal discomfort that lasted for some time. To my knowledge, no known cause was ever discovered. Looking back, I am sure that my mother was depressed because she was married at a fairly young age. She was overwhelmed with the care of three young children in addition to having to carry out endless housework. My father's attitude towards her did not help either. He treated her as a weakling and looked down upon her opinions as well as her intellectual ability.[60] He was a harsh critic and did not tolerate weakness of character or failure. After our dinner, instead of resting I remember her trying to finish her ironing, while my father would be paying attention to the news on the radio. He would be listening to the short wave radio with his eyes closed and his right hand on the tuner dial. Sometimes she would complain to him that he would not talk to her, but he would say that he was just resting his eyes.

Other times I would notice that she was crying silently while ironing in the evening. She would later complain that throughout life she had never been free or independent. During the early part of her life she was under the stern rule of her domineering four older sisters. They would tell her to keep quiet and that she was too young to have any opinions. She married young and lived with her mother in-law and sister in-law in the same household. They were both very domineering women as well. My aunt Knarig repeatedly reminded her that she had graduated from elementary school which my mother had not had the occasion of attending.

Life was difficult for a housewife in those days. Besides cooking food and handling the grocery shopping, which included

---

[60] One must consider the cultural setting at the time, where even physical spousal abuse was common. There was a certain expected behavior from the newlywed bride; she was not even allowed to speak to the other members of the family, unless she was addressed. Fortunately neither one of these conditions applied to my mother.

going to the butcher for fresh meat every day, she had to take care of the children's needs, sew and knit. In addition, there were seasonal chores such as making fruit jams by putting pans of jam covered with cheesecloth on the rooftop for it to thicken, preparing peppers, eggplants and okra to hang on a string to dry for winter use, making tomato and red pepper paste and similar tasks which took advantage of sunlight. Once a year, the wool in the pillows and the mattresses was washed and put on the roof to dry. Then it was beaten with a cane to make it fluffy before it was placed back where it belonged. I used to enjoy that first night of sleeping on the fluffiest soft mattress that would still be warm from the hot Aleppo sun. However I also remember a late summer storm which had blown in from the South with wind and rain when the wool had to be quickly picked up to prevent it from blowing into the neighbor's yard.

Fridays were wash days and a washer woman (the only help my mother had) would come to wash the clothes in a big boiling pot. The pot would be sitting on a small kerosene burner. It had to be balanced just right, otherwise it would topple over. Before we left for the U.S. in 1954, my father had bought an early model washing machine made in Germany with a separate small centrifuge on the side for the spinning cycle. The wash still had to be taken up to the roof to be hung to dry. Fortunately, the meal for Fridays was always simple, *Mudjettera* which was a healthy pilaf, a mixture of lentils and bulgur with some caramelized onion on top. Besides there would be no fresh meat available on that day, since in a Muslim country Friday being their holy day, there would not be any animal slaughter.

Once a year my father would buy a live turkey from the farmers who would be passing through Bustan Keleb with a flock of birds, while they were actively bargaining and selling them to the store owners. My father would be carrying the turkey by holding it from its feet. From the balcony, my mother would see him coming down

CHAPTER 7

the street and would dread it, because it meant a lot of additional work including cleaning and cooking the bird. Initially the turkey would be tied to the railing in an alcove by the kitchen and fed well. This included forcing it to swallow a whole walnut. On the day of the slaughter, my father would have the turkey swallow a jigger of Arak and then he would take it close to the drain under the kitchen sink; he would put the wings, one under each foot and slit the throat. My mother's ordeal would start after the slaughter. She had to pull out the feathers and then clean the viscera, saving the liver, the heart, and the gizzard to be later added to the rice pilaf stuffing. She also had to singe the fluff on the flame of the kerosene cooker. That smelled terrible, like burnt hair. It penetrated throughout the entire house and we had to go to the balcony to get fresh air. The turkey had to be cooked on a small kerosene cooker. The large pot had to be balanced well on top of a tripod. The kerosene cooker was temperamental at times; some impurities would be caught in its opening and it would start sputtering. One had to enlarge the nipple opening with a device that had a pin with a handle on it and frequently one had to pump the piston to increase the pressure in the reservoir.

We did not own a refrigerator; instead we had a cabinet with screened chambers located at the most breezy part of the house. This was only for things that would not spoil readily. All meals containing meat had to be cooked daily from fresh, newly slaughtered lambs. Milk and dairy products were consumed fresh daily. The milk had to be boiled after it was delivered to our home. During the summer when we had company, we would go to the grocer to buy a small block of ice for lemonade. The grocer would cut the ice with a hand saw and tie a rope from the hole in the center of the ice for us to take it home. We used to hold our hand under the shavings as he was sawing it to quench our thirst.

There were usually multiple street venders selling vegetables and fruits which were loaded on their donkeys or carts. They would sell it by the kilo which they weighed in a hand-held scale made of two baskets tied with ropes to a pole. One had to watch them carefully, since they would trick the housewife by pushing down with their thumb to make it look like your product weighed more. They also used rocks that had been worn down with repeated use, instead of officially certified brass weights. If you complained, they would take it personally, start an argument, get angry at you and curse profusely.

There were also ice cream and *gazoz* (soda) venders as well as people with their containers strapped on their back, selling *ayran* (tan), *soos,* and *demir-hindi* (the latter two were drinks made from plant roots). They would constantly yell trying to get the attention of their customers. Early in the morning, a man would be selling hot *sahleb* with cinnamon on it that smelled almost irresistible.

Early on, my father had forbidden me to buy any of these drinks. He had told me that they would be using the same cup for all their customers. The vendor would wipe the cup with a dirty rag hanging from his waist after each use. The rag had become brown with dirt. Father used to say, "Instead of cleaning it, he is dirtying it further."

The most irresistible smell from the street vendors was the one where a man would set up a small charcoal cooker and roast corn on the cob near my father's store. I would hesitate to ask father, but probably he would see me looking in that direction. He would give me two 5 piasters to get a corn husk for each one of us. The only other time he would yield to his desires and would admit it to me, was when on some early mornings he would send me to the *baklava* store to get two *burmas* for us to share.

* * *

I am amazed now more than ever that my mother, not having had any formal education, had self-taught herself how to read and write in Armenian. She was an avid reader of newspapers, especially

CHAPTER 7

serial novels published in weekly papers, as well as other books and the Bible. She had high regard for education and probably had been most influential in my pursuing a medical education. She would whisper in my ear while putting me to bed that if I studied hard, I could become a doctor. She studied English with a tutor before coming to the U.S.; she also took drivers education courses after she had been in this country for a year or two. She passed the abominable California driver's license test, but was reluctant to take the driving test, because she was afraid of the heavy traffic in the Los Angeles area.

She had high regard for cultural values; style and appearance were important for her. Most people who met her came away with the impression of having met a gracious lady. Her personality and demeanor were quite different from any of her sisters. She avoided confrontation and was even-handed and gentle.

Mother had a high regard for literature and classical music. I remember she had taken me to see the movies "Hamlet" with Laurence Olivier, and "Chopin." She would recognize the Chopin pieces on the radio and say, "Chopin, Chopin" similar to his teacher in the movie. The other movie that we had gone to see as a family that had greatly impressed me was, "The Stone Flower" to the music of Prokofiev. Produced by a Russian studio, it had a large number of symbolisms which prompted my father to speculate about Soviet Russian political aspirations.

*   *   *

In the late 1980s, my mother became aphasic after her stroke due to carotid stenosis, but did well until my father could not be managed at home due to his progressive dementia and falls. This was painful to witness in a person who was so mentally capable that he could detect an error of a few cents by the cashier at the grocery store.

LEAVING KAYSERI

We would visit my mom and dad every Friday evening with the kids while they lived in their condominium in Montrose. Once they were trying to tell us about a phone call they had received regarding their savings account at the bank. My mother remembered what it was, but was unable to get the right words out and my father did not remember what it was about. After ten minutes of sign language and shouting out the words, mother was able to convey to my father the message, who remembered to tell us what it was all about. Then he said, "Two of us seem to add up to one person." We all laughed.

After my father passed away, my mother moved to be with my older sister Arpiné and my brother in law Popkin. They both gave her the best care and attention they could. The other members of our extended family are grateful for their services.

My mother believed in education and had definite ideas about discipline and a strict moral code. She would use anecdotes to make a point. One of them that I remember well was about the Golden Bracelet. While a man was being robbed, he told the robber, "You can take all the money I have, but you cannot take away my golden bracelets." The robber looked at his wrists and did not find any bracelets. The man said, "The golden bracelet is my skill and knowledge that I have acquired through education, with which I can earn more money; but as to you, you will remain a robber forever."

The other anecdote had to do with a "know it all" newlywed bride who called on her neighbor to ask her about how to fix *dolma* (stuffed eggplants). At each step the bride told her, "I know, I know." Eventually, the neighbor got frustrated and said, "And you cover the top of the pot with a cow dung patty *(Tezzeck),*" which was used in villages for fuel. My mother felt strongly that one should admit ignorance and have the willingness to learn. This principle Alice and I had noted after repeated contact with people in the office during my medical practice. There were people with varying levels of insight. There was a group of people who were ignorant about a specific subject but would accept it and be willing to learn and change their point of view. Others thought that they knew it all and would not be willing to accept new ideas. We would call the latter group "The ones that did not know that they did not know." They were beyond help.

Her strict moral code came to the forefront when we had taken her to see the movie, "The Graduate" which was playing at the Army base while we were stationed in Maryland. She felt upset and was not forgiving regarding the negative values the movie depicted.

Near the end of her life, she lost her appetite and gradually succumbed, having lost a lot of weight. At an advanced age, it would have been unproductive to do extensive testing to diagnose the reason for her illness. If she was able to express herself, I am certain she would have refused any form of treatment. She kept pointing up to heaven when we used to go to visit her every Saturday. She faded away peacefully in the same fashion she lived her life.

Morning Chores

Besides being meticulous about cleanliness, my father was also particular about our diet. It must have been one of the responses he had developed to insure our survival, having lived through starvation and witnessing the death of his younger sister and baby brother. In the mornings, with a raw egg in his hand he would be waiting for us as we came out of the bathroom. He would have punched a small hole on both ends of the egg and applied salt and pepper to make it slightly more palatable. We were prompted to suck out the contents that would splash into our mouth as the yolk passed through the hole. He would block the hallway, so we had no choice but to swallow the raw egg before we could get to our rooms and get ready for school. He also would give us a soup-spoonful of cod liver oil with a small amount of lemon juice squeezed on top. My sister Shaké and I had a hard time digesting the fish oil. We would regurgitate it tasting the fishy-oil all morning long.

Typically, we had *Kete* with *khorez* in the center and jam, honey or *bekmez* on top of it with some cheese for breakfast. At times, my father would get fresh dates that came from Iraq on back of camels. He would cut them in half, take the seeds out, and then he would put some sweet white butter in the center and line them out like a fleet of "boats" for us to eat.

Rue Hamrah, Beirut

On our daily walks in the La Canada hills, "up and down" as Alice calls it, as we come up Hillcrest Avenue the neighbor at the corner has a bush of "rose geranium" by the roadside. We both stop and rub the leaves to smell the aroma. It always reminds me of the first time I had smelled it in the downstairs garden of my maternal aunt Arous's home in Beirut. The whole scene of that garden opens up in front of my eyes. We had gone to Lebanon to get away from the hot, windy, dry and dusty summers of Aleppo. It was basically a barren city except for a few parks and streets that had some greenery. In contrast, Beirut looked like a paradise to us with beautiful gardens surrounding the homes, with blossoming trees, bougainvillea, jasmine, and honeysuckle.

The smell of the geranium reminded me of the total experience, mainly pleasant, of the carefree days of childhood. Aunt Arous lived on the top floor of a two-story building that she rented from the Arab landowners. The upstairs unit had a fairly wide living room with tile floors that extended to a covered veranda overlooking the street. It was separated from the living room with a stained glass partition and doors. My maternal grandparents also

CHAPTER 7

lived there and I remember my grandfather, Yacoub Matossian usually sitting in the veranda and smoking his *nargila* (water pipe). The whiff of the tobacco smelled sweet on the breeze. He was a gentle person and was willing to engage in conversation. He used few words to express himself and usually we found him pensive and counting the beads on his *tasbeh* (oriental prayer beads). As children we did not realize that in the recent past, under the Turkish authoritarian government in Aintab, where he worked as the recorder of property deeds, he was forced to change the deeds of Armenian properties into Turkish ownership during the latter part of the deportations.[61] He had also tried to save a number of Armenian women who were separated from their family members from further deportation towards Deir el-Zor by vouching for them and later turning them over to the American orphanages.

Once he was having fairly severe back pain and had asked us the cousins to walk on his back to give him relief. I remember feeling his ribs and shoulder blades under my feet. Our ages were approximately 8 to 12 years old and we did not weigh much at the time since we were quite skinny. Once, however we had experimented by blowing into his water pipe and water had filled up in the tubing and we had run up to the roof not to be blamed for damaging it.

Aunt Arous kept some hens on the flat rooftop of the house to have a daily supply of fresh eggs. Her favorite hen was smaller than the rest and lay small, round brownish eggs and had found a special soft place in a wooden box filled with straw in the attic to lay them on, while the others lay their eggs on the roof in the dirt among their droppings.

---

[61] He also came across the title of the American Hospital and the Antep College properties which were originally under an Armenian's name since Americans could not own land directly. He changed them to the American Board of Missions' name so that they could maintain ownership and continue to operate. Source is the videotaped interview of Vahide Dekmejian by Armen Aroyan.

LEAVING KAYSERI

Sometimes my cousins and I would get to playing more lively games on the roof and some of the hens would be scared and fly down the side of the building to the field next door. We had to run after them to catch them to bring them back, before Aunt Arous would find out about it. We had to camouflage the cousin carrying the hen and prevent Aunt Arous from seeing the hen while we passed through the living room to get to the roof. Aunt Arous used to be quite temperamental and would get upset easily. We wanted to avoid that scenario if at all possible. We also built miniature replicas of Arab villagers' mud huts with sand. We built a small mound of dry sand, and then put a layer of wet sand on top of it. When the top layer dried, we emptied the loose sand inside carefully from an opening. Once we had "obtained" some cement from the street pavers and fashioned the covering of the hut with it. It seemed solid and indestructible; it probably lasted on the roof until the building was torn down to build tall apartments.

Playtime with my cousins used to be educational and challenging. One day Aunt Arous asked us to go to the nearby meat market to buy ground *kufta* meat. We got the meat in a flat pan and while we were walking home, Hrair asked what would happen to it if he turned the pan upside down. Of course Zaven and I said it would fall. Hrair thought that since it looked sticky, that it would not fall. Well, the meat landed on the sand. We had no money to get a new batch. Hrair scraped off as much of the sand as he could and turned the meat inside out so it looked fresh.

Screams of murder, accusations and retribution with gnashing of teeth started coming from the dining room as soon as the *kufta* was being tasted and sand was grinding between the teeth.

We were banished to the rooftop by Uncle Nerses and there would be no dinner for us that day!

* * *

During the summer of 1944, my maternal grandfather Yakoub Matossian, became ill and started vomiting blood. According to the medical custom of those days, he was kept at home in absolute bed rest and the physician would make daily house calls to check on him. To keep a record of his blood loss, Aunt Arous insisted on keeping all his vomitus in pans in the bathroom. She was concerned more than his physician about the severity of my grandfather's illness and tried to convince him by showing the amount of blood he was losing. The smell of old blood would fill up the house. We had to keep the windows open all the time and we spent more of our time outside on the veranda, but it still failed to convince his physician.

His condition got worse; he became unresponsive and was moved to el Kulliyeh-AUB hospital, but expired within one day. At that time Uncle Nerses was finishing his clinical years at the medical school.

"Shiralarda"

My mother did not know her exact birthdate, since the family bible containing all that information was lost during their deportation from Aintab. She was told she was born during *"şhiralarda"* in late summer, which meant that it was during the time grapes were harvested from the orchards. The grape juice was concentrated by boiling and later preserved as a sweet treat to be used during the winter months.

On one occasion, four families had gotten together for *shiré* in the courtyard of my Uncle Parsegh's house in Aleppo. All the preparations were made the day before, including the rental of the container used to stomp on the grapes, the press and the big pot that measured at least four feet in diameter and was used to boil the grape juice in. Early the following morning, four huge containers of white grape were delivered and all the children and young adults got into the act of stomping the grapes. The juice would flow down a spout into the pails and poured into the big pot on the fire. The

Washing the big pot to boil the grape juice. My Aunts holding it with help from my sister Shaké and my mother while my father is looking on.

Grape juice boiling to thicken for basdigh while being stirred and tasted.

fire was fueled mainly with the dried branches of the grapevines.

At the end, the left over pulp was put in the press so the last drop of the juice could be obtained. As the fluid started to boil, a sweet aroma permeated the air of the courtyard. Hence the name,

CHAPTER 7

Shiré, meaning sweet, from the Arabic root *"sharab"*. It is even used in the Romance languages to account for the word syrup.

After the juice was clarified with calcium bicarbonate powder, starch was slowly added to it and mixed thoroughly to convert it into a slightly thickened yellow paste that was spread as if someone was plastering it on a white sheet; next it was allowed to dry under the hot Aleppo sun. Later it was peeled off by wetting the back of the sheet and was dusted with powdered starch, folded and preserved for use as a fruit roll. It was called *Bastekh*, *Bastegh* or *Bastik* in Armenian. A fancier dessert was prepared with a roll of the *Bastik* with walnuts and a mixture of sugar and cinnamon and was folded in a triangular fashion.

As the grape juice kept boiling, it thickened and its color gradually turned golden brown. This was when the fresh shelled walnuts were strung on a string and were repeatedly dipped into the vat until enough layers of the fluid jelled on it. Then they were suspended from a stick to dry. This was called *Sujuk*. Further boiling made the fluid darker and thicker. This was mixed with some grain and poured into pans to dry and became *Tarkhana*. The final residue was poured into containers and was used as *Bekmez* (molasses).

This entire day's activity reenacted in a certain way is what my extended family lost when they left their homeland and their orchards in Aintab and Kayseri. They had tended and nursed those orchards like their forefathers had done before them. But now they found themselves in a temporary safe haven in a foreign country, within an Arab city, Aleppo, having arrived as a small number of survivors of the genocide in the desert. Getting together as an extended assemblage must have given them some sense of belonging and must have recreated what they had experienced as children.

LEAVING KAYSERI

Convicted to Hard Labor

My cousin Krikor Kitabjian and I were both named after my grandfather. My cousin was three years older than me; to differentiate us, he was called *Metz Koko* and I was called *Bzdig Koko*. This story came to my mind after he passed away in April of 2008.

Subsequent to my arrival in the U.S. on an immigrant visa, the Syrian government insisted in keeping in touch with me requesting my grades and performance reports from the school. This did not seem necessary since I was not on a student visa; thus my stay in the U.S. did not depend on my keeping up my grade point average up to a certain level. However they had more sinister reasons to keep in touch with me. It had to do with my military draft responsibility. When I left Aleppo, my father had vouched for my return, since I was seventeen and almost ready to be drafted. But three years after I had departed, my father had also emigrated to the U.S... He was fully willing to pay whatever sum that they required, but there was no mention of that until later when the Syrian authorities realized neither one of us were returning back. They had checked on us at the gas station on Ramadanieh, but since they could not trace either one of us, they posted my picture and name at the border crossings. It so happened that my cousin Krikor had gone to Aleppo from Beirut to see my grandmother. He was arrested on his return at the border, since he had the same name. After two hours of interrogation, with the help of his Arab friend with whom he was travelling, they finally released him.

I got an official document from the Syrian military soon after I graduated from college. It was a judgment against me from the military court martial where my case was taken in absentia. They found me guilty of failure to report to duty and I was condemned to four years of hard labor. After I had become a Naturalized citizen, I had written to the Syrian embassy in Washington D.C.

CHAPTER 7

that I wanted to relinquish my Syrian citizenship, since the U.S. constitution did not allow a person to have double citizenship at the time. They wrote back informing me that I could not do such a thing, since I was a Syrian citizen for life.

My father was happy that he had saved me from military duty, having known what hardships Armenian men had suffered in the Turkish Army. However he was quite upset when I was drafted into the U.S. Army during the Viet Nam war. Fortunately as an officer, I was treated well and did not see combat due to being kept in the U.S. mainland by the sheer ignorant decision of my commanding officer. That is a story for another day and another book.

(See Appendix for documents from Syria and U.S.)

Beirut, summer of 1945

We all had gone to Beirut for summer vacation. Usually summers in Aleppo were hot, dry, and windy. At times the wind would be strong enough to whip up all kinds of street trash, including dried horse manure, directing it towards our eyes and mouth. The summers in Beirut used to be humid, but we could go swimming in the Mediterranean; however more commonly we would go to the mountain villages. These were beautiful, wooded spots with a number of running springs and verdant valleys. They were mainly populated by Christian Arabs who had resisted Islamization by the Ottoman Turks during their 500 years of occupation and had managed to survive in the mountains of Lebanon. There were monasteries and churches hidden in some of these villages. In other village squares, they had monuments and statues commemorating certain heroes of past struggles.

I was introduced to hiking by an Armenian music teacher that lived in one of these villages. I had started taking piano lessons for the summer and my cousin Metz Koko was taking violin lessons.

My piano teacher knew most of the trails in that region. After familiarizing ourselves with the area, we took a couple of major hikes to a monastery and a forest. We were accompanied by Uncle Parsegh who was endowed with a good sense of humor, which made the hikes more enjoyable.

The hike to the monastery was fairly straightforward. It was down into a beautiful, verdant canyon until one reached the monastery. However, the native villagers' lacked a good sense of time and distance. We kept hiking all morning, but the canyon seemed endless. As we came upon a passerby, we would ask as to how far it was to the monastery; they would say, "Just a few kilometers more. It is just a short distance." By now we were getting tired and hungry. We stopped for an impromptu picnic in an apple orchard and there came the Arab owner. We thought he would be angry with us for using his shaded garden for our picnic. Instead, he turned out to be quite friendly and talked about his extensive land holdings and his Christian background. Somewhat later in the conversation, we realized that he wanted my sister Arpiné to marry his elder son and showed all the orchards that would be hers. My uncle Parsegh was the only adult male in our group. He had to be diplomatic in his answers and promised to respond to him after he had talked to my father. This was a ploy to get us out of the situation. We eventually got to the monastery and were served wheat pilaf by the Jesuit fathers. On our way back, we avoided the apple orchard's owner.

Our next hike was more harrowing. It was into a thick forest of pine trees in the Lebanese wilderness. The locals had warned my uncle about it and had recommended that he get a guide, since some people had gotten lost there. Two donkeys were hired to carry our supplies. It was a cloudy day and the trees had grown into each other covering the sky and obstructing our view from all sides. After some extensive hiking, we realized we were going in circles. The guide eventually admitted that he was lost also. Again,

CHAPTER 7

we took a break from hiking and had a picnic. The guide meanwhile did some checking to determine where we were. However since it was getting dark due to the thickening cloud cover above us, he thought it would be best if we cut across to reach the highway. We had to travel some distance to reach it. It was evening when all of a sudden we reached a clearing and found the road we were looking for right in front of us. We had no choice but to flag down a construction truck, which was returning after dumping some dirt by the roadside. We piled in the back of the truck to get back to the village. When we reached home and looked in the mirror, we did not recognize ourselves because we were completely covered with white dust.

A picnic in the apple orchards in the Lebanese mountains. Back row from the left; Aunt and Uncle Parsegh Kitabjian, their daughter Arousiag, Gregory Ketabgian, my sister Shake, my mother Beatrice making lentil kufteh and my sister Arpiné. Front row left, cousins Harutune holding an egg and cousin "Metz KoKo" Kitabjian on the right.

Chapter 8

Ramadanieh Gas Station

Following a city ordinance to move all gas stations to the outskirts of Aleppo for safety reasons, my father negotiated a lease with an Arab religious order to develop a corner lot in Ramadanieh section of the city. This was the final stop of the tramline from the Tilel section of town. The location was across a historic military hospital which is mentioned in the genocide memoirs of Virginia Meghrouni, named "Vergeen."[62] During World War I it was used to care for the wounded soldiers of the Turkish and German armies from the Palestinian and Bagdad fronts. As the fighting intensified, the number of casualties had increased and had overwhelmed the help. The majority of the physician and nursing staff were Armenians who had somehow survived the massacres and deportation to Deir el-Zor. When the British drove out the Turks from Aleppo, they took over the hospital and marked its roof with a red cross. I remember the cross remained there until the Syrian Arabs proclaimed independence, at which time it was changed back to the Red Crescent.

The property for my father's gas station was a chalk hill that rose gradually from the street level. The Boyamian cousins found a group of husky *Zeitoontsys* to dig the chalk hill to level it to clear the way for the construction to proceed. As they started digging into the hill, they ran into some old Muslim graves. To the dismay of my father, all construction came to a standstill until a Mullah could come and pray over the remains of the buried. They were eventually removed to another site at which point the construction once again resumed.

The gas station was a success since a lot of truck traffic passed

---

[62] Derderian, Mae. *Vergeen: A Survivor of the Armenian Genocide*. Los Angles; Atmus Press Publications, 1966. pp. 163-212.

CHAPTER 8

through the area to go to Qamishli,[63] a town where a lot of farming was done by Arab landowners. My father got an Arab named Ahmed to be the caretaker and night watchman of the gas station. He told us that he hired a Muslim for the position to avoid any type of sabotage which might have been brought about by the neighboring Arab population.

My father was fond of vegetation and for that reason grew some plants from raw *chedene,* commonly eaten salted seeds sold in dry goods stores. With daily watering, the plants grew tall, almost to the height of his shoulders. On one occasion, a truck driver wanted to know why he was growing Hashish on the side of his gas station and suggested he get rid of them before it was noticed by the authorities.

While watering his plants, my father had noticed that if the sun was behind him at a 45 degree angle, he could create a rainbow with a fine mist from the nozzle of his hose. When he showed it to Ahmed, he was awed but with the same breath he told my father to stop so that he would not get into trouble with the Muslim clerics, since in their faith only God could create a rainbow.

The old gas station in Bustan Keleb had manual gas pumps with two liter glass containers situated above the pump that would fill up with gas and then would empty to visually measure the amount of fuel delivered to the vehicle. The pump had a long handle which had to be moved from one side to the other repeatedly to pump the gas. I had to be 10 to 12 years old before I was tall and strong enough to pump it. My father had developed huge shoulder and forearm muscles from this daily labor of his. Initially his new gas station also had a manual pump which was later replaced by an electric pump and subterranean storage tanks were also added. The new station was mostly managed by my father's cousin Nazar, except for some weekends when my father took over.

---

[63] A small town in the northeastern corner of Syria, in a fertile agricultura district.

The Store on Bustan Keleb

My elementary school graduation ceremony from Gertasiratz School in 1950 in Aleppo included a short musical selection (Minuet in G by Beethoven). I was to play the piano and was accompanied by two classmates who played the violin. We practiced ardently under the guidance of one of our teachers. However we were not taught how to start playing the piece simultaneously. This fact, plus stage fright caused us to have a false start; otherwise once we had gotten started, we did well.

I was disappointed that my parents were not present for my graduation because they had to leave for Istanbul to accompany my sister Arpiné who was on her way to the United States. On the same occasion, my father also wanted to visit his cousins, the Benlians who lived in Istanbul.

During his absence, I was to look after the store in Bustan Keleb where he sold automotive oils and lubricants. The store had 50 gallon barrels full of different grades of oil and grease lining

The Ramadanieh gas station with the new electric pump with my proud father. The sign in Arabic, read from right to left, indicates the company name: "Socony-Vacuum", a subsidiary of Mobil Oil.

CHAPTER 8

the wall on the right. On the left were shelves filled with different cans of lubricants and grease of quart and gallon sizes. The lubricating oils were sold by volume and were measured with a one liter official measuring beaker. The city official had refused to give my father a half liter measuring container, but he had figured out a way of measuring it by tilting the liter container until one could see the top of the bottom rim. The grease was sold by weight and was weighed on a scale using brass weights. The floor had a thick layer of grease and dirt caked on it due to repeated drippings of the oil and foot traffic. Just to be useful, I would scrape off the grease during quiet periods, but in less than a week's time it would accumulate there again. I think the heavy shoes of the auto mechanics would drag in the dirt.

In addition to managing the store, on a weekly basis I was responsible for taking a deposit of two to three thousand Syrian pounds to the central office of Socony-Vacuum-Mobile Oil Company. This was necessary so that gas would be delivered to our gas station without any interruption. The secretaries and the workers at the Mobile Oil Company were surprised to see so much cash in the hands of a fourteen year old boy. My father had advised me to put the cash in a brown lunch bag so no one would suspect that I was carrying such a large amount of cash while I was on the tram.

My father had repeatedly stressed to me that to have gotten a well-rounded education, one had to first graduate from "the school of Bustan Keleb." This really meant to learn how to deal with people, and mainly **not to trust anyone**. It also gave me the chance to be exposed to a culture that I otherwise would not have gotten to know. Bustan Keleb was a microcosm of a large industrial park composed of Armenian artisans. In addition to garages and stores that sold auto parts, batteries and electric motors, there existed a whole series of shops that would repair anything that needed to be restored. At the time, imported new auto parts or electric motors were very expensive. Instead, there were shop mechanics that had the ability to reproduce any part of a machine with tool and die with lathe machinery. There were electric-motor rewiring specialists as well as battery repair specialists. As a child I would spend hours watching these mechanics work on their wares. To be able to deal efficiently with the customers, one also had to pick up some of the shop parlance of Bustan Keleb. People would come into my father's store asking for a specific type of oil replacement for their car or truck. We had to look it up on a list to find the correct product. The two words which I had come across that I could not find in the book were: "Dé Francais" which I later found out stood for "Differential" and "Jamsy" which stood for "GMC."

* * *

One day a truck driver came to the store to buy half a liter of motor oil. When I asked where his container was, he said to give him the oil in the officially certified measuring liter cup. I was not supposed to allow anyone to borrow it from the store; but the driver said, "See the truck down the street? I will put the oil in and return the container back to you." As I watched helplessly from the store, he put the oil in the engine, closed the hood, threw the container to the back of his truck, and drove away.

Baron Hotel

One end of Bustan Keleb Street ended at the Bab al Faraj (Lookout Gate of the old walled city) while through the western end one could see the Baron Hotel. This was the old historic hotel built in 1909 by an Armenian family. On his way from Turkey, their great grandfather had traveled through Aleppo and was heading towards Jerusalem to fulfill his lifelong dream of pilgrimage. Realizing that the travel accommodations for pilgrims were not ideal at the time, he decided to build a European style hotel.

CHAPTER 8

Throughout wars and revolutions, the ownership and management has still remained in the hands of the same family. Through the decades the Mazloumian family had seen kings, princes, criminals and writers pass through their hotel. The hotel guest-book had the names and signatures of a number of famous people. Lawrence of Arabia had slept in Room 202; from the balcony of Room 215, King Faisal had declared Syria's independence; and Sweden's King Gustaf Adolf, Egypt's Jamal Abdel Nasser and David Rockefeller of New York had occupied the presidential suit. Agatha Christie had written "Murder on the Orient Express" while sipping tea in the dining room of Baron Hotel.

During the Genocide of 1915, Cemal Pasha had taken over the Baron Hotel and the regular guests were moved to a building across the street. Hovannes Mazloumian was in charge of the hotel at that time and happened to be in good terms with Cemal Pasha. He knew all the officers and secretaries working with him and thereby was able to help a large number of Armenian deportees who landed in Aleppo to be directed south towards Hama or Damascus, a safer region than the desert road to Deir el-Zor.[64] Salih Zeki, the ruthless governor of Evereg-Kayseri and later of Deir el-Zor, also stayed there during his short tenure in Aleppo.

There was a less well known hotel next to my father's store, Hotel Carlton, which catered to lesser foreign personnel; we would recognize their nationalities by their uniforms and outfits as well as by the languages they spoke. Other street watchers would keep an eye on their consorts and visitors and make snide remarks. There was a casino on the eastern side of the street near "Bab al-Faraj." My father had admonished me from walking on the east side of the street since there were "dancing girls" in there that he did not want me to see. I remember looking carefully while

---

[64] Odian, Yervant. *Cursed Years*, 1914-1919.

walking on the western side where I could only see a dark space with some barely audible music emanating.

They Did Not Succeed: My father speaks:

> *We went to Aleppo and started working there…*
>
> *Even after immigrating all the way to the United States of America, I saw the same liars there again. They preached us peace; it is just a word in the dictionary. At this time I wonder if people know the true meaning of peace. I do not think so.*
>
> *During the First World War in 1914, Germany and Turkey were allies. What were Turks going to gain from the war? If Germany lost the war, Turkey was going to lose as well. The territories Turkey owned before the First World War were so extensive that Turkey was incapable of governing them.*
>
> **The Turk's main purpose was to eradicate the Armenian people and to get rid of the name "Armenian" from the face of the earth. They did not succeed and in the process hindered the progress of their country.** *They were never interested in the war. The reason they joined it was only to cleanse Turkey of Armenians.*[65]*They had lots of problems because of the presence of the Armenians in their midst. England and France used Armenians as an excuse to interfere with the internal affairs of Turkey. They benefited each time that the Armenians were killed. When Turkey was busy during the massacres, it lost Iraq, Syria, Lebanon, Egypt, Saudi Arabia, as well as all of their oil wells. They woke up to realize this, but it was too late.*

---

[65] The Armenian engineers who were working on the constructions of the tunnels on the railroad systems were being deported to Deir el-Zor; the German military personnel complained to the Turkish officials that they were undermining the progress of the railroad line to Bagdad. The Turkish top officials refused to defer their deportation.

CHAPTER 8

The life of an Armenian has always been miserable. But this time, after four years of war and wretchedness, one and a half million Armenians were lost. Immediately after the war, God woke up. He pitied us a little bit and had the Russians help these poor people. The Armenians fought hard to defend themselves. At the end they were able to have a small country, not the kind they wanted. However we do not know what the future will bring. We have to be patient and wait. We know that we want to be free. The time will come. Independence is impossible now. When it happens, we will not be able to govern ourselves. There are more populous nations than us that are not independent; where would we fit in this equation? I wish the intelligent people of our nation would use their brains and not mislead the general public.

The Piano

A recent picture published of a black upright piano with brass candlestick holders on each side, reminded me of the piano we had in our home in Aleppo. It belonged to my aunt, Uncle Haig's wife Arpiné. They had recently married in 1945; as a bride, the piano was her only possession.

My father had suggested that they allow the piano to be moved to our house on a temporary basis for us to practice on, since no one was using it in their home. My father also used to help my younger Uncle Haig financially, since he was unable to work due to his visual disability. When I first started taking lessons, I used to go to their home to practice. But this did not seem very practical.

I remember how hard the Armenian *hammals* (porters) worked to get the heavy piano up three flights of narrow stairs to our apartment. I used to wonder about these *hammals;* how they managed to carry these heavy loads on their backs. I knew what they ate; it consisted of bread, onions and some cucumbers, I used to see them while they rested in the shade of a wall near my father's Bustan Keleb store. They were extremely poor and I don't think they ever got out of their predicament, considering what they got paid for their services.

I had started taking piano lessons while we were on a vacation in the Lebanese Mountains. After returning to Aleppo, my piano teacher was a nun at the French Catholic School called "Immaculate Conception" where my sisters were students. The lessons were very boring; they consisted mainly of numerous finger exercises and the repetition of chords. It was called the Hohner method. Besides, now that I look back, we had a problem with communication. The nun spoke French and Arabic, which were my two poorest languages. I was not motivated to practice. The only piece that I wanted to work on was a Spanish dance on sheet music, La Paloma, which my teacher had provided. I remember I had made her happy when I played that piece well. As I got older, I was no longer permitted to enter the Convent school.

My next piano teacher was a famous pianist who came from Soviet Bulgaria. I could not remember her name but I found an article in the "Hai Antep" periodical about her and her husband, the famous *kemancha* player, Kemanchist Roupen.[66] I recall him sitting in the living room of their home with his kemancha and asking me if I could make the piano sing like a bird, which he could with his kemancha. Other than not being able to do that, I could not even play the scales to his wife, Azniv Manougian's satisfaction. She was an unhappy and often angry woman who told me that everything I had learned up till then was all wrong. I was holding my hands either too high or too low. She would hold a long ruler under my fingers to keep them at a certain height, and if it was not the right height, she would bang on my knuckles hard with her ruler.

---

[66] *Hai Antep*, The Union of Armenians of Aintep in America Inc.

CHAPTER 8

Once, my parents had invited my piano teacher and her husband to our house for the evening. My father actually wanted to hear her play the piano. After some urging, she reluctantly got up to play. However after hitting a few notes, she let out a scream scaring us all and hurried to get off the bench, saying that the piano was awfully out of tune and she could not play it. I could see the disappointment on my father's face. Naturally, after that incident I did not continue with my lessons much longer. In spite of all this, my father would not give up on me.

By then, the piano had been moved back to its previous location, Uncle Haig's residence. In its place my father had decided to buy me an accordion, since it was a popular musical instrument at the time. Besides, I could practice it at home. This coincided with my sister Arpine's immigration to the U.S., where she arranged a correspondence course for me. It was exciting at the beginning, but after getting to the level of playing slow Viennese waltzes, which I had transposed from the piano score, the novelty soon wore off.

I do not know what happened to the piano when Uncle Haig and his family emigrated to Soviet Armenia. I should ask my cousin Aram in Apovyan, Armenia about it.

Soot

Although it rarely snowed, the winters used to be quite cold in Aleppo. Most of the houses were heated with free standing, coal-burning stoves. The pipes that eventually took the smoke outdoors, circled the room and finally went out the window. Burning coal was a fairly dirty process. Besides creating a thick smoke, the soot often blocked the pipes.

My father tried an innovative idea of burning diesel fuel in the same stove. He had a five gallon can set up high on the adjacent wall with a small faucet that dripped the fuel into a funnel which was connected to a tube that conveyed it to the stove. It had a round container with a sieve-like cage on top. Except for the persistent smell of the diesel fuel in the room, it worked very well generating plenty of heat, to the point that it would turn our stove bright red. It was easy to regulate the amount of heat generated by counting the number of drops of fuel dripping into the funnel per minute.

However after a few weeks of this new experiment, the smoke started to back up into the room. Upon undoing the exhaust pipes, my father found out that they were all full of round fluffy soot that floated and settled covering the whole living room furniture, including the carpeting. It was very hard to get the soot off of anything it settled on. The experiment was discontinued to the obvious satisfaction of my mother.

* * *

One night, all of us children woke up around midnight with a splitting headache associated with nausea and vomiting. Our grandmother, Arous Ana was babysitting us while my parents were in Beirut for the evaluation of my mother's illness. Our grandmother, in her great effort to keep us warm on a cold winter night, had made a charcoal fire in a *mangal* (brazier). After the flames and smoke had subsided, she had brought it into the living room and opened our bedroom doors. I am sure we all had the early stages of carbon monoxide poisoning!

Around bedtime we would warm up a brick block on the stove; we would put it in a flannel bag and take it into our bed with us to keep us warm. My maternal aunt Rahel used to have a *"tander"*, which essentially was an elevated table with a brazier under it with seats surrounding it and a blanket that covered the legs and laps of the occupants. This would keep the family warm while they worked or studied at the table.

CHAPTER 8

Kitabjian cousins in Aleppo in 1950 before they were all dispersed to the far corners of this earth.

Chapter 9

Coming to America: My father continues his journey:

> *In 1950, Arpiné started on her journey to America. In 1954, Shaké and Krikor began their travel and in 1957, Beatrice and I went all the way to California by the Pacific Ocean. I searched for a place where my wife, my children and I could live a peaceful life. I had a prosperous business but I left everything behind, including the Muslim countries.*

Leaving Beirut

It was a cold, wintery day in late January in Beirut. It was similar to the many cold days of the winter which Beirutsis refused to admit existed. Most of the houses did not even have heating units at the time and people did not own many winter clothes. It was a city that was tuned to enjoy the pleasant Mediterranean climate during the summer with outdoor cafes, restaurants and beaches.

My sister Shaké and I had gone there with our parents to embark on an ocean liner, Excambion, to immigrate to the U.S. after our quotas had come up at the U.S. Embassy. My parents could not accompany us, since their quotas had to be obtained from Turkey where they were born.

This was 1954. Syria was evolving into socialism with multiple military coups. Due to this, the schools were closed most of the year. Usually we would be bussed to school in the morning. But the school gates would be barred by politically active Muslim students who would announce that we had to march back down the hill, to the center of town to demonstrate. We would be forced to march chanting the name of the popular politician of the day.

CHAPTER 9

Family portrait of Artin Kitabjian with Arous Ana in 1950, Aleppo, Syria.

Practically none of the Armenian and Christian Arab students were involved or even interested in the local politics of the time. We were more interested in completing our education and moving on with our lives. Therefore as soon as we would get to the city streets, we would bolt and run back home; although some of the Muslim Arabs at times would pursue us. Because most of us were fast runners, usually we would manage to outrun them.

* * *

It started raining harder as we got to the wharf in Beirut. My parents came into our cabin to bid us farewell. It was the first time I had seen my father shed tears. Most of the time he was stern, serious and would never show any emotion, especially in public. He would usually express his displeasure to some unacceptable behavior on our part with a stern look or frown. He used to say,

"Without speaking a word, you should know what I want." Actually he was not a very demanding man. Most afternoons on weekends or after dinner, he would peel apples and oranges for everyone; at times during summer he would peel purple carrots and share them with us. On other occasions, he would wash romaine lettuce which we would eat together on the balcony.

Our aunts and cousins had also come to the wharf to wave us goodbye, but the incessant rain had made the typical "Bon Voyage" scene impossible.

The ship was a cruise liner but also carried merchandise in its hull. All the passengers were wealthy Americans who had embarked on a Mediterranean cruise. They were mainly into playing cards; "Canasta" was the rage at that time. They were reading, eating and drinking. Dancing at night was their only exercise.

When the American passengers found out that we were immigrating to the U.S., they were very excited and interested in us, since in those days there were not a large number of immigrants heading towards the U.S.

A couple with two children came on board from Alexandria, Egypt. They were returning home after two years of service in the U.S. Embassy in Cairo. Initially they asked my sister, Shaké to babysit their children while they were dancing at night. Later they became more interested and questioned us about the reasons why we had decided to emigrate and wanted to know what our future plans were.

As soon as the ship left the port, both my sister and I felt seasick with nausea and dizziness. The waves looked quite angry. The water was churning and seemed muddy due to the silt from the Nile delta. We had to take Dramamine tablets that made us very sleepy and forced us to go to bed. When we woke up, we did not

CHAPTER 9

know how much time had elapsed. It might have been a whole day or longer by the time the cabin steward came in to clean our bathroom; he was surprised that we had not left our room. Meanwhile my sister Shaké, having an unstable stomach, was still throwing up; she had to get additional Dramamine from the ship's doctor, since we had run out of our own supply.

The next day, although I was still somewhat dizzy, I decided to go up to the dining room. I realized that getting out of the cabin and having some food could help me. However after studying the elaborate menu, I still did not understand what was being served. The descriptions of the dishes were all in French. It was high-French cuisine with heavy creamy sauces. I had not had any exposure to these kinds of dishes in the past. Fortunately the waiter assigned to our table was a kind Greek who spoke a little bit of Arabic and English. He was willing to bring me any dish I desired to try to see if I could stomach it. We were not used to eating heavy meals or large pieces of meat, especially if they were rare or undercooked. I went down to tell my sister of my adventure and tried to coax her to come with me for the next meal.

At each port of call, the tourists were taking shore excursions and sightseeing trips. We were somewhat reluctant to spend our father's hard-earned cash which he had given us before leaving Beirut. However when we got to Piraeus-Athens, we thought we should take a short excursion to see the sights. Also when we had reached Naples, we went to see Pompeii. Due to my being underage, the tour guide was reluctant to allow me to see the room with paintings of sexual positions in Pompei. However after a moment of vacillation, he agreed to allow me to come along. I didn't think the drawings in a small, dark room under the stairs were that revealing.

The most exciting event at each port of disembarkation was the late arrival of the chef from his latest love object. We were told he had a lover at each port and would get drunk and not wake up early enough to get to the ship on time. The crew would get the ship all ready to cast off the ropes but would wait with the last plank for him to get up to the lower hatch when a speeding taxi would make a screeching stop at the pier. Everyone would be watching and cheering as this short, fat Spaniard got out of the taxi while still kissing his lover and teetering to go up the plank to disappear into the ship's deep insides. We all wondered what the dinner would taste like that evening.

At Marseille, the ship was unloading U.S. made Chevrolet cars. As we were passing by the longshoremen, we heard them speaking Armenian and started talking with them; when they found out that we were also Armenian and emigrating to the U.S., they were very happy for us and considered us lucky and expressed their desire to do the same, if they could find a way.

This sentiment was also expressed in Aleppo and Beirut. When my classmates at Aleppo College found out that I was leaving for the U.S., they all came and congratulated me and expressed their wish to do the same.[67]

* * *

After leaving the Azores, we hit a Northern Atlantic storm which the captain assured us he was trying to avoid; but it turned out to be one of the most exciting and harrowing experiences of our lives. After the second day, the waves started to build up and the swells were as high as the ship's front deck and were washing over the bow. Because there was not much cargo for ballast in the hull, the ship got tossed around by the ocean waves. After all, they had only

---

[67] Many years later, Uncle Popkin's brother, Armen and wife met a physician active in Armenian affairs in Chicago, Raffi Hovanessian, who was one of my classmates at Aleppo College.

CHAPTER 9

taken in a few bales of cotton from Alexandria. The bow of the ship would rise up with one swell, then for a few seconds it would feel like it was suspended weightless in space; then it would come down with a crash. During these episodes all the bolts and steel joints would be stretched to their limit and it would sound like the ship was breaking in two.

All this shaking and jostling got a lot of people sea-sick and there was again a run on the medical facility for additional Dramamine. It seemed that the ship was ill-prepared for this type of a severe storm. I remember the grand piano in the dance hall was sliding from one corner of the room to the other and smashing against the walls until it was tied down with ropes. In the dining room they had wetted the table matting and there were retractable edges that were lifted up to prevent the dishes and glasses from sliding off the tables. But the crystal water and wine glasses would still slide to the edge hit it and topple over and break.

It was impossible to sleep with all this noise; every one of the drawers from the dressers was falling out. After a while we realized the rolling sounds were the fruits on the table that had fallen to the floor.

Following four days of stormy weather, we reached the safety of Boston harbor. The immigration intake point was in New York. There was no security check at the port of Boston. My father had written to his cousin Garabed Mouradian, the only survivor of his family from the Genocide, to meet us but we had no point of contact. I decided to take a walk up the harbor. As I walked by and passed an older gentleman, we both stopped and looked at each other; then he said, "Are you Krikor, Artin's son?"

We got together on the ship for coffee and we told him about our parents. He had come to the U.S. before the Genocide and had kept in touch with my father.

The American couple from the U.S. Embassy in Cairo had wanted to treat us for our first meal in the US. We went to the Boston Commons area with them and had clam chowder and fried scallops. Ever since then when I see scallops on the menu, I think of these people's generosity and desire to create good will, especially towards new immigrants. They found out that I was bringing my Hohner accordion. They wanted me to play it for all the passengers one night, since there was not much evening entertainment on the ship except for piped elevator music, which after a few days we had learned by heart. My accordion repertoire was limited to slow waltzes and some classical pieces. After I reluctantly played all I knew, I think they had expected some fast polkas and fireworks. It all ended with some cool applause.

The next memorable experience at the end of the cruise was when we approached New York harbor to dock at Hoboken in New Jersey. As we approached the Statue of Liberty, my sister and I realized that the other passengers had all turned around to see what our reaction would be upon seeing it for the first time.

It was impressive, but we were reserved and did not jump up and down. They all congratulated us and wished us good luck, which was very touching.

*   *   *

My uncle Nerses met us at the customs in Hoboken-New Jersey harbor. We had brought with us a whole list of his requests from my father. This included mostly edibles he could not get in the U.S. at that time. It included mostly roasted nuts and seeds,

CHAPTER 9

chedene and *leblebu*.[68] In addition, we had a shining brass samovar for him. The customs officer opened up the luggage and came up with the chedene seeds and asked, "What is this?" My uncle mentioned the name, but the customs officer had never heard of it. Uncle said it was edible and he offered him some, but the officer refused, nonetheless he let it pass. Then the question of my accordion came up. They claimed that it was made in Germany and not allowed to enter the U.S. After a lengthy discussion, because it was for personal use and not for trade, it also passed the customs.

As we were driving back from New Jersey and passing through the Lincoln Tunnel, my uncle allowed a peek into his personal view of life in the U.S. "As you pass through this tunnel, there is no turning back. You will be stuck in this country for good; you will be forced to work till the end of your life and never feel satisfied or happy that you have accomplished anything. You have fallen into a trap and you do not know it," he commented.

My sister Shaké and I looked at each other, but we did not completely understand the full ramification of what he was saying. We were young, ambitious and had just arrived in the U.S. Everyone else we knew back home was dreaming of coming here. His statement has more meaning for us now after a lifetime of hard work and exposure to all the trials and tribulations that life threw at us. At the time we did not have any idea what his personal life was like. We found out soon enough after getting to their home in Hamden, Connecticut.

---

[68] Roasted seeds commonly sold in the Middle East, e.g. chick peas, watermelon seeds and sunflower seeds.

LEAVING KAYSERI

Hamden High, February 1954

I was walking down the main hall of Hamden High School in New Haven, Connecticut to register for classes as a transfer student from Aleppo College, when I noticed that all the students in the hall stopped necking and gossiping and watched my entry. My father, knowing that the East Coast would be cold at that time of the year, had me tailored for a woolen suit and a full length overcoat. The usual attire at all-boys Aleppo College would also have included a white shirt and a tie.

As I looked around to see what the other students were wearing, I saw T-shirts, jeans, leather jackets with fur collars. I must have stood out as a foreigner. I became "The Boy from Syria." That afternoon when my sister Shaké came home from work, I told her that we needed to go shopping to get T shirts and jeans for me so I could fit in.

It was hard to convince the principal's office that my real name was Krikor Kitabjian,[69] since Syrian Arabs had translated it into Karkour Ketabgian from the Arabic derivation of *kitab* to *ketab*, meaning book, into English phonetically. Later on while becoming a naturalized citizen, I had my name officially changed to its present form, since all my other school records were under that name.

When my father saw my name placed on the office door of 65 N. Madison, Pasadena, for the practice of medicine with my uncle Nerses Matossian, he was upset. He thought that by changing the spelling of my name and by not including Artin for my middle name, I was denying my relationship to my family. Of course, nothing could have been further from the truth. This was partially

---

[69] The family name Kitabjian was given to our ancestor, Harutune Euredjian (born 1810) who was a scribe who registered vital information for the city government. He kept the book, Kitab in Turkish from Arabic roots; thus the name. Their original name was Euredjian when they had immigrated from Hadjin to Kayseri in 1750s.

rectified by my daughter Ani, giving her son Noah Math, Artin as his middle name, but my father was not around by then to notice it. As "The Boy from Syria," I became a popular tool for the teachers of geography and social studies courses in the school. I had to give a short talk and demonstration of Arabic and Armenian writing and speech and fielded questions concerning life and education in the Middle East. It was obvious from the questions that the average student in high school in the United States lacked the background information, especially in history and geography. This was quite different from the way we were educated in Aleppo, where we were exposed to a large variety of courses and languages from eight AM until five PM. When it was time to give me credit for all the courses which appeared on my transcripts, the school official in Hamden High did not have enough room on his form to register them. The teachers were also impressed with the general information that I had been exposed to. In spite of not having mastered all the irregular verbs, the French teacher gave me a good grade, because he appreciated my strong background in classical music. The history teacher was so impressed with my background in European history that one day he had me conduct a class in his absence, but the students became unruly and rebellious and gave me a hard time.

Poetry in Elementary School

We were given a poem to memorize for the spring of each year, which we had to recite in front of the class. Those who recited it well were then chosen to represent the class in front of combined classes of a number of Armenian schools. I had a problem of memorizing any poem and would freeze in front of the whole class. That was until my last year in elementary school. I had found a simple poem in English, possibly by Rudyard Kipling for children, "Try, try again," Somehow I had no difficulty and was allowed to recite it in front of the whole school.

Talking about poetry reminds me of an incident in elementary school when we were studying a poem by Taniel Varoujan.[70] The teacher wanted us to cross out the word "breast" and substitute it with the word "chest." This is where the poet says: "I raise my arms to Goddess Anahid's breasts." It goes to illustrate how restrictive the teaching was at the time and what changes having taken place within the last 60 years. Of course all of us started smirking when we came to that erased word.

*   *   *

We had several teachers in Gertasiratz Elementary school in Aleppo who manifested their personalities with the type of corporal punishment that they doled out. One was a tall young man who lined up three wooden rulers together. He had the culprit hold his hand out and gave him five to ten strokes, depending on the infraction. Another teacher was a stout man who would put his fat hand on the edge of his desk and ask you to bring your ear between his big thumb and forefinger for him to squeeze and roll it back and forth. The most unusual form of punishment was a grimace from the teacher to allow the students who sat behind the unruly one to flog him when he least expected it. Unfortunately I was a common recipient of these different forms of punishment, which might have been due to a degree to my boredom during classes.

*   *   *

According to Syrian regulations, the city provided the teachers of the Arabic language. We had an unusual teacher who talked to himself while walking down the narrow streets near the school, while he dragged his fingers on the walls. He never looked up and looked at you while talking. He did not know any Armenian and

---

[70] Taniel Varoujan (1884-1915) one of the major Armenian poets of early 20th century who was arrested, deported away from Constantinople on April 24th and killed with a large number of other intellectuals signaling the start of the Armenian Genocide.

we did not know much Arabic except for the street language and cusswords, of which the Arabic language had ample examples. The sessions mainly involved getting up and reading passages from the textbook. Neither he nor most of us were interested in understanding the subject matter. Furthermore it was difficult to look up the words in a dictionary. This later became an additional factor in our desire to leave the country. I remember the last day of our school year when for the first time he looked directly at us and gave a short lecture concerning our existence as Armenian Christians in a Muslim country. He wanted to know why we lived in Syria since he said the government, the police, and the judges were all Muslim and we really had no rights. He thought that we should convert to the Islamic faith. Then we realized that when he was talking to himself while walking, he was actually repeating passages from the Koran.

The most pleasant class we had was taught by Levon Khoja, who used to teach us Armenian songs by writing the words on the blackboard and giving us the tune that went along with the words. He used to pucker his lips and use his index finger to show how big the mouth should open for the best tone. Besides some patriotic songs, he also taught us several of the classic old songs.

Tzitzernag:(Swallow) was one of them.
        (Song of an Exiled Son) by K.A. Totokhiantzi
        translated from the Armenian by Gregory Ketabgian.

                Tzitzernag, Tzitzernag,
                Beautiful bird of spring
                Tell me, where do you fly
                So swiftly.

                Fly, swallow
                To my birthplace, Ashdarag,
                Build your nest
                Under the Armenian roof.

LEAVING KAYSERI

Skokie, Illinois

After spending the spring of 1954 with Uncle Nerses and his wife Ruth, I felt both homesick and oppressed because of the adverse environment in their home. On my sister Shake's suggestion, I took a railroad trip to Chicago to spend the summer with my sister Arpiné and her husband Popkin. The atmosphere there was quite different from that in Hamden. Popkin and Arpiné treated me as an equal and included me in all of their activities. These included outdoor concerts, ball games, family get-togethers and Sunday dinners at Popkin's folks' home on the Southside of Chicago. My sister Arpiné was excited to have both of her siblings staying with them. After Shaké arrived for her summer vacation, it was decided that she should return to New Haven to break the news to Uncle Nerses regarding leaving her job and moving to Chicago as well.

The house in Skokie was a newly-constructed tract home on the edge of the Midwestern prairie. The upstairs bedroom and bathroom were unfinished and the backyard was not landscaped. We decided to lay wooden flooring and to insulate the walls, so I could use it as a bedroom. While we were moving the wood for the flooring upstairs, Armen, Popkin's younger brother who had come to help us, slipped and fell. One of his legs had gone through the plaster board of the ceiling of the downstairs hallway. We extricated him with some difficulty. Fortunately, he did not suffer any serious injury.

To complete my senior year, I had my records transferred to Niles Township High School in Skokie. Most of my teachers in that high school appreciated my varied background; the students were more down to earth compared to the rich kid syndrome I had experienced in Hamden High.

*   *   *

CHAPTER 9

I had a friend named Tom Geer from an upper middleclass family who had a car and a driver's license, which was a rare thing in those days. The car was a Henry J, made by Kaiser-Fraser Company, a small company that had started to build motor cars after WWII, but does not exist anymore. It was fairly rudimentary with a simple engine and a manual gear shift.

Tom Geer liked to drive around, go to coffee shops to smoke cigarettes, drink coffee and play the juke box. Whenever his parents were away from home, he would get drunk on hard liquor; he had discovered where his father had hidden the hard liquor in their garage. One night after we had gone to the neighborhood pizza parlor, we went to his home and started drinking whiskey, usually chasing it down with some beer. My limit was one shot of whiskey and one beer and by then I would start becoming nauseated. I lost count of his intake of liquor by late evening when he started passing out. While I was trying to get him into bed, he started vomiting the evening's meal. After the vomiting had subsided, I pulled out the sheets and took them to the laundry area and cleaned the floors. I waited for his parents to show up, but it was past midnight and they had not returned yet. I left them a note to check on him and walked home. The note said, "Tom had a little too much to drink. Please check on him." The following day he was upset with me about the note because apparently he was punished.

Skokie being not too far from the Wisconsin state line, most of the high school senior students would drive up on the interstate highway towards Milwaukee to get some beer to drink, since the legal drinking age in Wisconsin was 18 while it was still 21 in Illinois. We could see the huge signs of all the beer companies lit up with neon lights claiming to be the best beer of Wisconsin: Schlitz, Pabst, Hamm's and so on. There would also be advertisements of beer on some of the windows of the houses visible from the highway. To make a few extra dollars over the weekend, an elderly woman would serve the kids beer in her living room with no questions asked, while everyone watched Lucy and Desi Arnaz on her television.

On another occasion, Tom Geer had a friend come along with us to get some beer, a John S., who I later found out did not have a good reputation at school. It was a cold wintry night and there was snow on the ground. Henry J did not have a defroster; we had to scrape off the ice from the inside of the windshield to be able to see where we were going. John had Tom drive to the back of a liquor store and waited for him in the alley. Next we saw John at the back door of the liquor store running to the car with a case of beer in his arms and the store owner waiving his fist in the air and shouting.

John quickly threw the case to the back of the car and we drove off. Some distance away, the car skidded and went into a ditch by the side of the road. We went down into the ditch to push the car back up so it would be on the road again. No matter how hard we tried, we were unable to push the car back on the road. While we were pushing the car, as I looked up from the gutter, I saw a police car with its lights flashing stop near us. I could see my whole future plans ruined if I was arrested for burglary. I could even be deported back to Syria.

The police wanted to know what we were doing.

"Driving around," we said.

After helping us get back on the road, he checked the inside of the car. We were holding our breath while he was going through the seats, but he did not pull forward the back-rests of the seats; he only directed his flashlight and did not see the case of beer. The Henry J did not have a trunk. It had a hatchback and one had to pull the back-rest forward to get to it.

After I started college Tom and I saw each other less often, mainly because of my heavy academic load. Once he tried to set me up with his mother's hairdresser who had recently come to the

U.S. from Germany, thinking that we may have something in common; but I was too involved with premed courses to be interested. John wanted to be an FBI agent all his life and started at a local junior college for his requirements.

* * *

One of the most interesting courses I was required to take during my premed training was Comparative Anatomy. Among other animals, we had to dissect a shark and a cat. I used to take some of these animals home to the basement for further dissection. It created a great deal of interest and curiosity, especially on Popkin's part who wanted to show it to all his guests, despite its nasty formaldehyde smell. The smell assured me that I would always have an unoccupied seat next to me on the "L" train while going back and forth to school at Navy Pier, before the Western campus of the University of Illinois was built.

Summer of 1955 and Jobs

I had to get a driver's license the day before my high school prom. We were offered a driver's education course in high school before graduation, although we had to learn it on standard shift cars. I had practiced with Uncle Poppy in his dark blue 1950 Mercury sedan that had faded after being parked outside in the Chicago cold winters and hot and humid summers.

I had volunteered to sell tickets during the lunch hour in the school cafeteria for the prom, but people kept asking me if I was going to it and with whom. I had decided to do some volunteer work since I was advised to get involved in student activities before applying for college. The sale of prom tickets was the only activity left for me to do because everything else was taken. I had not even thought about going to the prom, nor did I have any particular person in mind to ask.

Few days before the prom, I gathered enough nerve to ask a girl that was not too popular in class. I remember that she constantly talked about her father's job at the Rand McNally Map Company. Fortunately she agreed to come. At that point it became crucial for me to go through with the DMV to get my license.

The examiner was a gruff, skinny old man who did not speak much, but asked me to drive, make turns and park. However the acid test was to back up into someone's narrow driveway. This was more difficult, since the back window of the Mercury was small and the view on both sides was limited as the cars at that time did not have right side-view mirrors.

The first time I tried it, the car ended up on the grass. The second time, I was on the edging.

"Give up," he said, "You'll never make it."

"No, wait," I said. "I can do it." The third time was a success.

The examiner grumbled and then said reluctantly, "OK, you pass but you should practice backing-up more often."

* * *

That summer Uncle Poppy would allow me to drive him and my two sisters to the local train stop to catch the train to Chicago. Then I would drive to my summer job at Naxon Utilities, a washing machine and electric frying-pan manufacturer.

It was difficult to find a job that summer as most employers were looking for people with previous experience. I had taken this job in desperation, trying to make some money before going to college to cover my book expenses. I did not feel that it was right for me to ask my father to pay for it, since the exchange rate between the Syrian pound and the US dollar was pretty steep.

CHAPTER 9

I am sure the pay was below minimum wage with no benefits, since it was a part-time summer job. Considering the risks involved, the compensation was not worth it. But I was young and inexperienced.

I was assigned to the punch press operation. It consisted of these constantly rotating heavy wheels at the ceiling level called flywheels, which when engaged with the push of a pedal, activated a heavy weighted mechanism called the press to come down with its full force on the tool and die encasement where a sheet metal was placed to be bent, bored or shaped, depending what the die under it demanded.

When it was in operation a banging noise used to shake the floor, which I am sure has contributed to my loss of hearing high frequency tones in addition to causing the constant ringing in my ears. This process generated a great deal of heat. To prevent the metal from sticking to the die, I had to apply used motor oil on each piece of sheet metal before I pushed the pedal. The force of the impact would send out a fine, linear spray of dark oil in all directions, including mine. This spray would be directed exactly at my chest level. Each day I would go home with my white T-shirts completely stained at the chest level.

The dangerous environment of my job became very clear to me when the foreman, a nice, short, older Italian man with broken and heavy accented English came to impress upon me the need to be extremely careful when the press came down. Most of the machines had a safety device that would sweep down in front of the press right before the press came down to take away one's hands out of danger in case one forgot due to inattention. However some of the units were older and their safety device to protect the worker was damaged. Furthermore the repetitiveness of the task throughout the day would hypnotize one as well as make him extremely bored and prone to daydreaming. When the foreman showed his two hands, I stood up and paid attention. **He had lost**

all his fingers up to the knuckles on both of his hands in the not too distant past. I assumed that he got an automatic promotion to a foreman's job after that.

Most of the other workers were young men without any secondary education, with no goals in life. They would be constantly gossiping about their sexual escapades and other macho activities of the weekend and would stop work repeatedly to light their cigarettes, while I was working and concentrating on the demands of the job. After about two weeks at work, the foreman came and checked the counter on top of the press and realized that I was doing about twice as much work as the others. He said, "You better slow down. You know, the price of the product depends partly on how fast it is produced; otherwise the people in the office will be confused."

I was definitely convinced when one of the younger workers came behind me in the parking lot, put his hand on my shoulder and shook me as he whispered that I was making them look bad, that this was their permanent job while I was working as a "temp" and a bad accident could happen to me if I persisted.

*   *   *

The following summer I decided to look for a different job that was safer, cleaner and where I could learn something in the process. Again jobs were hard to come by and everywhere, "No Help Wanted" signs were displayed. There were two drug company plants in the neighborhood. The first one was Searle, which did not want to see me. The other one was Wyeth. Although there was a "No Help Wanted" sign in front of the building, I told the secretary that I am a premed student in college and plan to apply to medical school and wanted to work in their lab doing research. The secretary was quick to point out that they did not have a lab on the premises and their unit was a redistribution center. But at that moment the foreman came in and said that they had an opening

CHAPTER 9

in the shipping department and asked me if I would be interested.

The shipping orders would come in; the pharmacist would fill them by putting them on the trays on a conveyer belt which would come to the packers to be packed. After choosing the appropriate cardboard box and taping its bottom, we would cover the bottles with sawdust filled paddings, tape the box, put the address label on and place it back on the conveyer belt to be taken to the delivery trucks for shipment.

The job was relatively clean, fairly easy and paid better than my previous job, since the foreman had placed me on the union pay scale of $1.25/hr.

Most of the workers were older here and more civilized than at my previous job. But their conversation mainly dealt with their immediate goals and what they planned to do on weekends and or on their vacations. Their educational level was fairly low and besides sports and television shows of the previous evening, there was not much to talk about. They could not wait for the workday to be over to line up at the time clock with their cards in their hands ready to punch out within seconds, so they could be the first one to leave for home.

Having watched them, I realized that they had nothing better to look forward to in their lives, which further convinced me to go ahead with my education to try to achieve more in life.

Leaving Chicago on "Route 66"

During the summer of 1957 my sister Arpiné, Uncle Poppy and I left Chicago for Los Angeles, California. The only direct highway available at the time was "Route 66," which was the route that destitute farmers and other people looking for jobs in California took during the early part of the 20th Century. This highway was also the one taken during the time of the Great Depression, the Great War effort of WWII and the Dust Bowl. John Steinbeck in his book "Grapes of Wrath" called this road that had become a migration path to the west, "the mother road, the road of flight." They had left to get away from the Midwest and the plains, while we were going to California for a better future and to continue on our family's westward movement and to resume our **journey of one hundred years**. My parents and my sister Shaké were already established there with the help of our maternal uncles, Hagop and Sarkis Matossians. My father had us buy a new 1957 Chevrolet for us to drive it to Los Angeles as well as to use it for the future. It was cheaper to buy a car in Chicago at the time, since we did not have to pay an additional transfer fee.

Now "Route 66" is considered a historic highway since it was so vital during the events of the last century. Of course we did not realize this at that time. Neither did we realize that within a few years it was going to be replaced by the Interstate Highway system. "Route 66" would be left to deteriorate, as well as the little towns and establishments along the way that depended for their livelihood on the passing parade of travelers.

The highway was built in 1926. It was 2400 miles of open road, mainly one lane in each direction. This made passing a slow farm equipment hazardous, let alone seeing an oncoming vehicle approaching you head on at a high speed and realizing that it does not have enough space to get back into his lane. There were many instances when we had to pull over on the shoulder and stop, to allow a speeding car to pass.

The boredom of the drive was interrupted from time to time when the highway passed through a small town. We were convinced that the highway was planned in such a way that almost all of the towns in the region were included on the route. Each town had its city hall with a flag pole and across from it would be the courthouse and the school. It was imperative to slow down to the posted speed limit as you passed through these towns, usually 10 mph; otherwise the highway patrol was ready and waiting by the city hall to give you a ticket.

CHAPTER 9

As we came further west, the scenery became more exciting and we tried to take advantage of it by briefly stopping as we did at the Grand Canyon. We did not realize how hot the Arizona-California desert would get during the summer. Although we always had an early start before sunrise, as soon as the sun came up, the heat became intolerable. We did not have the luxury of air conditioning at the time. We would get some ice from the gas station which would help my sister prepare cold wet towels to apply around the driver's neck to keep him conscious.

It was the desire to join our family members, to get on with our goals in life, as well as to see the sights of Southern California which motivated us to charge ahead.

Chapter 10

Uncle Parsegh

Uncle Parsegh, the middle son of Grandmother Arous, was a fairly amiable man who was more relaxed than my father and one who usually saw the funny side of life. Having been through the genocide at a younger age and perhaps less affected by it, he may have taken a more relaxed approach to life. He worked as a silversmith while we lived in Aleppo. At times when I went to his shop with an errand, he would be very eager to get me something to drink. It would usually be lemonade, which I needed during the hot Aleppo summers, especially after having walked the long distance to his store. He would have me turn the handle for the fan to stoke the fire, which was used to melt the silver and it was subsequently poured into the sand filled forms to get the sterling silver forks, spoons and knife handles. I used to watch him and his workers get these utensils out of the forms and cool them in a pail of water at which time they made a loud hissing sound. They would next file their rough edges; polish them carefully before they would put them for sale. The other types of silverware they made consisted of small forks and candy dishes made of fine silver wire that was worked into a design in the handles and was filigreed. That was more difficult to make and it took a longer time for someone to master it. For this purpose they used a small flame controlled with their breath through a tube in their mouth that directed the flame to melt the silver wire to weld it in place according to the design. They worked over a partially open drawer of their workbench, which caught the silver filings while they polished the finished product. The filings were later combined and melted with other silver pieces to make additional objects.

 His wife Aunt Knarig was an educated woman, since her father was a priest and she had graduated from Haigazian Elementary

School in Aleppo and had taught there for two years. She appreciated the value of education and was always congratulating me and encouraging me to continue on. Her gifts for my birthdays were usually books and once she had given me an ink pen with a silver filigree handle made by my uncle, which I have kept to this day. However her most unforgettable present for my graduation was a Kilo of chocolate bars. I kept them in the secret drawer of my desk and tasted small portions every day after dinner.

Uncle Parsegh was also full of funny statements and observations. Once we had gone on vacation to the villages by the mountains in Lebanon. When we checked out the rental home, he noticed that it also had a back door. He said, "Good, this way if the thieves come from the front door, we can escape through the back door."

On one occasion, the flies inside the house became numerous. He called all the kids and promised to give each of us a fresh almond for each fly that we caught. Having had adequate practice at school, we were quite adept at catching flies. He stopped after 10-15 flies, since he ran out of almonds.

On another occasion, he cut a rope into pieces and had each one of us hold one end of the rope and gave each one of us a secret word that we had to shout out when he pulled our rope. He had ingeniously given words that would have a different and humorous meaning depending where it was used in the sentence.

Boredom and Mischief

My cousin Zaven reminded me recently about some of the mischief we had gotten into while we were living on the top floor of the three story apartment building that had a flat roof. We used to get up there frequently when adults were visiting, because we would be free there to do whatever we wanted. At times we would throw pebbles from there at the horses of the carriages parked in front of the house or would drip soapy water on the parked cars.

My cousin Zaven especially remembered our rubbing a wire on the short wave radio antenna while my father and his guests were trying to listen to some important news about the war from BBC. This act must have caused an amazing amount of interference. This used to be common in those days with short wave radios. But on one occasion, my father realized that we were on the roof, ran up and saw us committing the crime; he was very angry and was almost ready to throw us over the edge of the roof.

The other mischief that I remember we used to get into was to take some matches and scrape off the material from the tip of the matchsticks into the opening of an old fashioned tube-key and then find a nail that would fit in it. We would tie these two to the opposite ends of a string and hit the nail against the wall. The material would explode like a firecracker. No children were harmed during this experiment.

Book of Poems on the March

As with all deportees, it was a difficult decision to know what to take along on the deportation march, not knowing how long it was going to be, where they were going and when they would get back home, if ever. My father had taken an Armenian dictionary which was a fairly large book plus a book of essays and poems of famous Armenian writers. As the march wore on and additional difficulties developed, he felt he could no longer carry these books and sold them to a grocer in the camp for a few gurushes (cents). Few days later, he found out that the grocer was using its large pages for the purpose of wrapping dry goods. To the amazement of the grocer, my father bought the two books back from him for the same price.

The family Bible that was fairly large and heavy and contained all the birthdates and other vital information was left with his maternal grandmother, who had stayed behind. She had remarried

CHAPTER 10

an Armenian Catholic. At the beginning of the deportations Catholics were not being exiled.

My father did not remember what his birth date was, since in those days they only entered the year – 1897 – on identity cards (*Nufus Keghati*). When he immigrated to the U.S., all official forms required a month and a day to be entered in addition to the year. He had adopted my birthday including the month and the day as his, so that he would remember it in the future. Later on, some people wondered how both father and son could be born on the same day and month.

* * *

Outside of the Deir el-Zor camp, my father was asked by a Mr. H., who was very ill and close to death, to take care of a notebook that contained some of his poems and memoirs and give it to his daughter from whom he was separated during the deportation march. My father had kept this notebook for over 40 years until 1957. When the time came to decide what he would bring to the States while emigrating, the notebook was given to my uncle Haig, who had remained in Aleppo.

In addition to this notebook, there were also papers that included stocks that my grandfather had bought with his profits from selling some of their handiwork as jewelers. He had taken a trip to Constantinople two years before the deportations, undertaking a fairly high amount of risk. There always was a danger of being exposed to bandits on the road. Therefore, not to jeopardize his life and possessions, he had bought stocks, which were safer to travel with than money in gold pieces.

While living in Aleppo, a large collection of books and memorabilia had accumulated through the years. These included the old ID cards from Turkey, the *Tapu* (deed) of the houses in Gesaria and Talas. The latter must have been given to my Uncle Parsegh, since it surfaced in Boston in an envelope that also contained Aunt Knarig's genealogy tree.

The rest of the papers, including everyone's ID cards, were destroyed by Uncle Haig's son Aram in 1957. This was due to false rumors that Turks who had amassed a large number of troops on the border with Syria because of a water rights dispute, were going to attack Syria and if they found any Armenians with connections to Turkey, they would kill them. This was a false rumor and it never materialized.

Later on in California, my father met a neighbor of Mrs. Eve Melkonian in Altadena, a Mrs. Bishop, who after some questioning happened to be the long lost daughter of Mr. H. She had survived the massacres in an orphanage and had later emigrated to the U.S. at a young age.

"Nerkacht", Repatriation

"Your motherland wants you; migrate to Armenia; we have made provisions for you: homes, jobs and land." So read the placards and billboards pasted all over town by the Soviet Armenian government in early 1946. They were willing to transport anyone by ship to Batum, Georgia free. From there, they would travel by rail to Armenia.

This caused a great stir in Armenian circles throughout the Middle East and Europe. Many people considered going, if they could convince the rest of their family members to go along with them. People dissatisfied on account of living as minorities in a Muslim country were tempted to repatriate, as well as those with great yearning to return to the homeland they had been dreaming about for years. Although there existed basic cultural and linguistic differences between Armenians living in the Middle East and Europe compared to Armenians living in the Caucasus.

Special organizations were set up to implement the task of repatriation. Prominent people hailing from each province of Western Armenia were chosen to compile and submit lists of those who intended to repatriate. My father was chosen to oversee the list for the Gesaratsies. I remember people used to come to our home in the evenings to get their names on the list, or to try to move their name up on the list, since they were eager to go as soon as possible.

During these visits there were discussions as to the safety and wisdom of their move to Soviet Armenia. All news and mail were censored by the Soviet authorities; it was hard to get an accurate reading of the life situation in Soviet Armenia. It was comparable to Shakespeare's definition of death, where no one had yet returned from the other side for us to know what to expect. But the Soviet propaganda machine was very effective for those people who wanted to believe what they were told.

My father was also tempted to emigrate but was cautious. He wanted additional information before making a final decision. My Uncle Haig who had four young boys and was unable to make a good living due to his visual disability, thought that if he went, the government would educate his children free and additionally he would get some type of a disability income.[71]

I remember my father had a meeting with a distant relative who was leaving with the next shipload of immigrants. They wanted to set a secret code so the repatriate could write to my father about the conditions in Armenia before he would make up his mind to leave. This person was a fairly wealthy jeweler who sold all his possessions and bought three disassembled GMC trucks to take with him to do vegetable farming in the Armenian countryside. He was planning to use his trucks to bring vegetables to town to sell them.

---

[71] Haig Kitabjian with his family of four boys and his wife left Syria from Latakia harbor to Armenia on November 1965 on the Russian ship named "Latvia." During the period of 1962-1982, total of 31,920 were repatriated from Iran and 4,848 from Syria, and smaller numbers from other Middle Eastern countries. Initial repatriation during the years of 1946 to 1949 was a total number of 89,688. Between the years of 1921- 1936, 42,283 were repatriated.

My father waited and waited before he could make up his mind; but no letter ever arrived. He said, "This is worse than a derogatory letter. We are not going." Later on we found out that this person last saw his trucks being unloaded from the ship in Batum and being confiscated by the authorities. When he asked as to what happened to his trucks, they had told him, "Now the trucks belong to the state." He became very depressed because he was responsible for his entire family's departure from Syria. He was jailed for speaking against the regime and apparently died in jail. Other dissidents were sent to Siberian Gulags, some with their families.[72] My wife Alice's uncle from France went through similar experiences after repatriation.

We found out later that all the immigrants were poorly treated. The government had no additional resources to care for the newcomers who were placed in poorly-heated tenement houses. Food and appliances were in short supply and the immigrants were discriminated against by the natives who were already suffering from shortages brought about by the war. They called the newcomers, "Aghber," meaning "brother" in a derogatory way.[73]

New towns were eventually built and named after the old regions of Eastern Turkey and Cilicia. This was a halfhearted effort by the Communist regime to make the newcomers feel more at home. But this did not make life any easier; actually it isolated them further from the life in Yerevan, the capital of Armenia. It is believed that the repatriation was a scheme worked out by the politicians in Armenia to give them increased political power and to avoid Armenian territory from being absorbed by Azerbaijan and Georgia. Others state that it was a way of replacing the population loss during World War II due to a disproportionate number of military losses of young men that Armenia

---

[72] See Armine Carapetian Koundakjian, *The Repression of Armenian Repatriates During the Stalin Era.* Yerevan, 2012. (Self-published).

[73] "Aghb" meaning dirt or garbage.

sustained.74 There were numerous monuments erected to honor these soldiers lost during the war which we saw during our visit to the Republic of Armenia in 2007. There was also a promise by Stalin that if Armenia was able to increase its population significantly with immigrants, Russia was willing to occupy the easternmost parts of Turkey, Kars and Ardahan and would allow the Armenians to rehabilitate these regions. However the immigration plan was halted early and the Turkish lands promised to Armenia never materialized.75

It was after travel restrictions were liberalized, following the death of Stalin in 1953 that we found out what life was like for these poor people. Besides having to wait in line in the cold weather for bread and other food items, they had to wait months to get appliances. They had waiting lists for everything. When my uncle Haig went repeatedly to find out about his standing on the waiting list for a refrigerator, his name was always at the bottom of the list. Later he found out that he had to pay graft money under the table to the person in charge of the list so his name could be advanced to the top.

Alice's aunt, who had emigrated from France, had a similar experience in managing to get anything other than gristle from the butcher, who always claimed that he had run out of good cuts. One

---

[74] Large number of the Red Army forces that were sent to the front lines at the onset of the German invasion of Russia was composed of other ethnic people from the Soviet Republics except for Georgia, which was favored by Stalin, since he was a native Georgian.

[75] **Pobeda**, the Russian ship that took repatriates from Beirut and Marseilles to Batum, on one of its trips from Egypt, while going through the Black Sea, had a disastrous and mysterious fire on board that killed 42 people on September 1, 1948. After that event Stalin revoked the order for further repatriations and the total repatriates had come to 89,688 instead of the projected 360,000. The fire was blamed on American spies among the Armenians. The incident had international political overtones beyond Armenia, since among the victims was a Chinese Warlord General, Feng Yu-hsiang or Feng Yuxiang, who was considered to be the only legitimate rival to Mao Tse-Tung (Main reference is James Sheridan: *Chinese Warlord: Career of Feng Yu-hsiang.* Stanford Univ. Press, 1966). Realizing a Dream, Then and Now. *AGBU Magazine*, Vol. 20, No. 2, Nov. 2010, p. 6.

day Uncle Tateos, while visiting from France, ran into the butcher and after giving him some gifts asked him why his relative could not get choice cuts of meat. The butcher told him, "Let her come to the back door for the better cuts."

The emigration had its deleterious effects in Aleppo also. Besides disrupting families and businesses, people were selling their homes in Nor-Kugh which was a predominantly Armenian part of Aleppo. Consequently the prices of real estate dropped. Later these homes were bought by Muslim Arabs. Soon after that, the Arabs erected a mosque right in the middle of the town square across the street from the Armenian Church. It had a minaret and a loudspeaker with the muezzin calling the faithful to prayer five times a day, including early dawn and late at night. This created racial tension and ill feelings among the two groups. The Armenians still living there expressed their displeasure with vandalism and smearing of feces on the door of the mosque. The mosque came to be known as "Stalin's Shaft" (*Stalinin kazığhi*).

Following the relaxation of emigration restrictions in Soviet Armenia, numerous immigrant families left the country to return to the Diaspora. These people could not tolerate the communist restrictions after having seen and experienced freedom in open societies in the Middle East, Western Europe and the U.S. After Armenia's independence in 1991, there has been significant brain drain due to the lack of jobs and shortcomings in governance.

One of the curbs on their freedom that the immigrants experienced was the suppression of religious belief and subsequently the reduced number of churches which were allowed to function. The Soviet authorities, besides pressuring the use of Russian as the official language, also enforced atheism, which constitutes cultural genocide. This became very obvious during our recent visit to the Republic of Armenia in 2007. We came across churches that had not had any services or maintenance for the last seventy years. We were shown two historic churches in the center of Yerevan where they were essentially surrounded by stores and tall apartment buildings on all sides so that the churches would not be visible by the passersby from the street.

We went to a village (Mrkashad) that had an old church with a partially destroyed side wall, where the roof was ready to collapse at any time with holes in it through which birds were freely flying in and out. *Badarak* (Mass) was celebrated once a year when Father Sarkis Petoyan from San Francisco came to visit the church. At that time there were not enough priests available to service all of the existing churches.

After Armenia's independence, a third genocide is essentially taking place by Mormons, Pentecostals and other sects who have come to preach their faith to attract poor Armenians offering them food and other amenities to steal their souls. The last two generations have grown up without any exposure to religious teaching by the Armenian Church. If these sects succeed in their mission, our battles and martyrdom through the ages of trying to stay Christian would have been fought in vain.

While visiting our Kitabchyan cousins in Abovyan outside of Yerevan, we took a walk towards the center of town. We saw the rusting, abandoned buildings of the factories that had been left vacant after the independence of the Republic of Armenia. The factory my cousins worked in had a large mosaic portrait of Khachadour Abovyan above the entrance. We were also shown a brand new church being built. This was once a factory town that was built during the Soviet occupation where no old churches existed. Cousin Henry was involved in carving new *Khatchkars* that have been placed in some prominent places. Cousin Levon is carving obsidian statuettes and religious pendants. Cousin Aram has been involved in collecting historic stamps and coins dealing with Armenian history. Most of the income for their families appeared to be earned by the wives of Krikor and Aram, working as a hair dresser and an artist, and the latter as a teacher.

Think Wisely: Here my father advises us on how to proceed in the future:

> *Initially they had the Geneva Peace Conference and now they have a United Nations meeting in New York. These two organizations, what did they accomplish until now to benefit the smaller nations? At their meetings they allowed the representatives of all nations, including the smaller ones, to speak out. Thinking that we said something at the meeting, we happily returned home. But we were deceived. This was a ploy on the part of the big nations. Mistakenly, we applauded them. Woe to us.*
>
> *We had no other recourse other than to depend on the big nations and we will be continuing in the same path. Nations with a population of ten to twenty million, which one of these are independent? They are all dependent on each other. Everything takes time. We need to be patient. All nations want to be independent; but now we are with the Soviet government. If we insist too much about being an independent nation, it is possible that we may also lose the small place that we have.*
>
> *As I have been contemplating throughout my life, I do not expect to experience anything substantially different from what I have seen during these eighty years. We Armenians, we never think wisely. The British, the French and the Germans have played many games on small nations like us for their profit. Now America and Russia are in the forefront. What a pity for the small nations that have hoped and waited for help from these big governments. If as a nation you are not strong and powerful, be quiet, and be happy for what you have. The words independence and*

CHAPTER 10

peace have been used by the powerful countries for their own benefit, and to fool the simpletons. The only independent nation is Turkey and no other government can say anything to it; it has taken all the big nations in the palm of its hand; it fools them and plays games with them.

Since the day I was born, the Armenian people have been constantly subjected to torture in the hands of the Turkish government. During my lifetime, the Armenian nation has experienced it all and it is written in our history books. Now my family and I have escaped to the U.S. so that we will no longer see the face of the Turks.

Even then, as a nation we have not been sheltered. Cyprus, Lebanon, Egypt, Syria, Iran, Iraq and Turkey, most of these are Muslim governments. The Armenian nation is spread throughout these countries and has suffered all kinds of difficulties and deportations. We all have not been saved, since only a few families have emigrated to safety but the majority still remains in these torturous conditions. The Armenians considered the Turkish government a sick and backwards nation. But we were mistaken; we see our enemy to be very insignificant; that is the problem.

Besides, we do not think intelligently. Where is Armenia situated? We all need to join that strong nation. Besides, we insisted on being Christian and insisted on depending on the liar Christian nations. Politics has nothing to do with religion. We presume that the Turks are sitting with their hands folded. No, look! Wherever there are Armenians, there the Turk is active and does not sleep. He is awake like a fox. Furthermore, there are Christian nations behind him. If you're not powerful, you always get the beating. We can make a statement by killing some consul here and there. But the whole world becomes our enemy. We do not want to depend on the Christian nations. We have tried it long enough. We need to accept our neighbor, the Russian government as our guardian and let us not lose Armenia.

I am afraid that one day we may still lose Armenia. The Muslim countries are all around us. Turkey is very much alive. One day it may yet play another trick on us.

A large number of Armenians repatriated to Armenia and then left. Life in Armenia has changed. They ran there with great enthusiasm saying, "Armenia, Armenia." Now we wonder why they are leaving.

We harmed our country with our own hands. The world is all mixed up at the present. It can improve or get worse. Only the future will tell.

Civil War in Beirut, Lebanon

(This section was written as it was narrated to me by my cousin, Harout Parsegh Kitabjian and his wife Rosine).

It was towards the end of 1974 when the war started. We had just gotten engaged to be married in February of 1975. At the time we were living in the Zarif section of Beirut, which was not too far from the St. Nichan Armenian Church, one of the oldest and largest churches in Beirut. That section of town had become more populated with Muslim families than it was in the past. This was due to the increase of the number of Muslim Arabs in Lebanon in 1968, after the Palestinian refugees were settled in camps near Beirut.

We lived on the top floor of a four-story apartment-building, and we could hear the bullets and the bombs whistling above our heads while we were trying to sleep at night. We had no protection and we had to go to the lower levels, where Rosine's aunt lived so we could get some rest. The Christian militia was shooting at the Muslim side of town where we lived.

CHAPTER 10

The composition of the population in Lebanon had significantly changed since the French Mandate was eliminated at the end of WWII. The predominantly Maronite Christian population had lost its majority and the Muslim factions wanted more representation in the makeup of the government. The constitution was set so there would be a Christian President with a Muslim Vice President with predetermined parliamentary representation.

As the fighting escalated, we started to have additional difficulties due to the lack of running water and electricity. We had to go and wait in line for water and bread as well as other food items. Water would be delivered to our section of town with a tank truck and people would line up with their pails to get it. We had to use the water for cooking, bathing and washing our dishes. Then we had to save the dishwater to flush the feces down the toilet. Christian fighters had occupied a tall building on the line of fire and they were shooting directly at us with snipers. At times they would bomb stores or bakeries where people had congregated while they were waiting in line. I will have to say that our Muslim neighbors were good to us and sometimes would bring the bread to our apartment after it was baked so we would not get fired upon while waiting in line.

Initially we had propane tanks for cooking, but later that became unavailable and we had to resort to kerosene burners for the preparation of our meals.

I was not able to go to work as a maintenance worker and mixer in a food processing plant any longer, because I was not able to reach my workplace. Later the plant I was working at had closed down due to the lack of supplies.

Eventually we decided to take a chance and make a run to a safer Christian section of town, Eshrefiyeh. There was a section that was considered to be safe for crossing; thus we made an attempt to get across with my Volkswagen. We somehow made it there in spite of the constant gunfire. At times I had to drive on the sidewalk or wherever there was open space on the road.

At the beginning my mother was with us in the Muslim section of town and while there, she would package some of our belongings and send them to the Christian side through couriers who were willing to take the risk of crossing the "blue line of fire," of course with the payment of graft. Later, my mother went to Tripoli to stay with my older brother and his wife.

My sister and her husband were able to get their visas to immigrate to the US in June of 1976. We were waiting for ours but they were difficult to get since there was no US embassy in Beirut and all paperwork was being conducted through the embassy in Cyprus. Fortunately the Armenian secretaries that worked in the embassy would find out who would be next in line for a visa to the US and would announce their names at the end of an Armenian radio program from Cyprus. We used to listen to this program every Sunday. On one of these occasions, we heard our name being read, so we quickly left for Cyprus where we waited a month to get our visas. We came to New York on December 2, 1976 and to LA on December 6th of the same year. It was on the following March that our son Shahé was born in Glendale, California.

My older brother, Metz Koko and his family were in Tripoli and had a great deal of difficulty as well. My brother was in charge of managing a sugar factory in the city of Tripoli, Lebanon. They were importing raw red beet extract and were converting it into pure white sugar. As the war progressed, they could not any longer obtain raw beet extract to purify, therefore the plant was shut down. Until they could get immigrant visas for themselves, for income, my brother ran a Xerox copying and key duplicating service. For a long time, they could not get a visa for their daughter, although their two sons had managed to arrive in the US earlier and were living in the Boston suburbs while working as goldsmiths.

CHAPTER 10

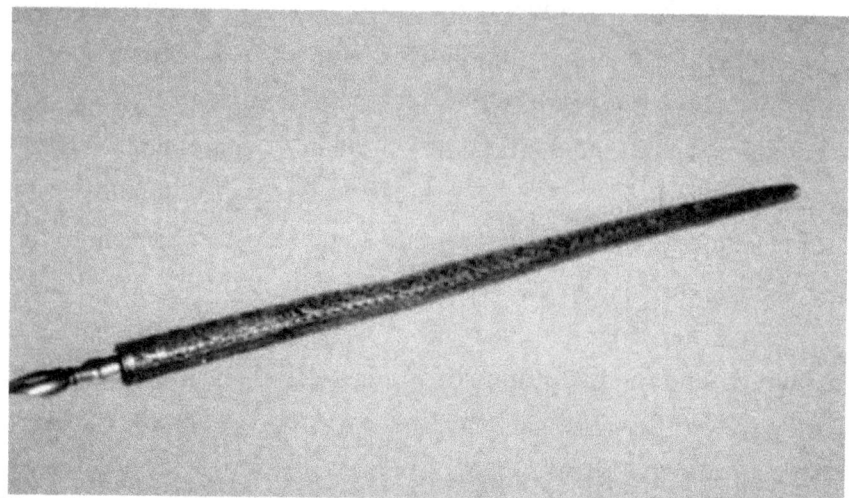

Silver fillegree pen that was given to me as my graduation gift from elementary school handcrafted by my Uncle Parsegh.

Fillegree spoon and fork by Uncle Parsegh.

LEAVING KAYSERI

1-ին էտապ 1919թ.   2-րդ էտապ 1919թ. 1 մարտի   3-րդ էտապ 1919թ. 1

4-րդ էտապ 1919թ. 1 ապրիլ   5-րդ էտապ 1919թ. 23 մայիս   6-րդ էտապ 192

7-րդ էտապ 1938թ. 2 հոկտեմբեր   8-րդ էտապ 1939թ. 11 հուլիս, գործածվել է 11

9-րդ էտապ 1939թ. 22 հուլիս, գործածվել է մեկ օր

Cilician-Armenia history told by stamps provided by Aram Kitabchyan from Republic of Armenia, son of Uncle Haig, stating the dates of printing and circulation. How the Ottoman, French, Syrian and later Turkish stamps were marked to be used in occupied regions as noted by him by the dates of their usage.

CHAPTER 10

Henry Kitabchyan in front of a Khatchkar he carved for his father's grave.

Levon Kitabchyan's multiple carvings on obsidian from Aragatz Mountain.

CHAPTER 10

Genealogy tree created by Knarig Kitabjian (Parsegh) in 1987.

A fillegree candy dish by Uncle Parsegh.

Chapter 11

The Armenian Language: Father continues to speak:

We have often been tricked by these big governments. We have sustained major losses because of them. They have deceived us repeatedly. Let us give up on our expectation of others to be doing things for us. Let us think for ourselves; what we can do for the Armenian nation that is scattered all over the world. We have to protect them from being assimilated and the Armenian language from being lost. The Mesrobian letters, the wealth that we have in our hands is a treasure that is not found anywhere else. We better appreciate its value. Let us try not to lose it. This endeavor starts at home. Therefore, let us go back fifty years; let the fathers and the mothers speak Armenian at home. We have to teach our children to speak Armenian as their first language. If we have Armenian speaking parents at home, then their children will learn the language very readily.

To be able to communicate with the general public, they certainly have to learn the language of the country. Learning two languages is not a difficult task. People who have come from Syria, Lebanon and Greece usually know three, four or five languages. They have found it necessary to learn them. The more languages you know, the more valuable you are. The world is getting smaller. Travel has increased. No one is sitting at home any longer. While traveling abroad, would it not be better to know the language of the country you are visiting? You will certainly enjoy it more.

CHAPTER 11

The Last Armenian

On a barren mountaintop looking
Among ancient boulders
Old glaciers having melted
Revealing remnants from the past.

Looking among the ruins
Among ancient carved stones
As if hurled asunder
By giants, by history.

Looking for the last word
A whisper, a word
For our perpetuity
From our forefathers
Who died willingly
For their God.

But the loud Babel,
Freeway traffic
And pounding Afro music
From the valley
Was blocking the faint sound
That was on the breeze.

He knew that being
The last Armenian
The responsibility fell
On his two shoulders.

He bent down close
To a boulder with a faint
Cross that had been carved
By an artisan thousand years ago.

As he put his ears close to the stone
He heard faint sounds
To Armenian Church songs

And he could identify
"Der Voghormia, Der Voghormia".
("God have mercy, God have mercy".)

Then he heard the spirit talking distinctly
But in Armenian which he could not understand,
A foreign language to him
Which he had not mastered
In spite of his grandmother's efforts.

What did the spirit say?
Build another church?
Stay pure to the end?
Return to your roots?
Return to your homeland ?

Gregory Ketabgian, 2010

The Future:

Returning to the subject of what to expect from Turkey and what they owe us, not that they are willing; let us assume Turkey gave the lands back to us. Who is willing to go there? And can we live with the Turks? Something similar to the Berlin Wall needs to be built in the middle and we do not have the resources for it. For now, let us be satisfied with the present condition. Let us not deceive our nation with empty promises. There is a right time for everything. Leave this nation alone. Let this nation take a little breather after experiencing one peril after another. Let it take a rest and prosper. If we are observant, the time is right and the opportunity arrives, then we can create a new Sardarabad.[76] Otherwise by simply asking, we will not get

---

[76] The Battle of Sardarabad (Armavir) was the last stand of the Armenian Republic against the Turkish Army in 1918 which was trying to occupy the land that present Armenia rests on. It enabled the existence of the present Republic of Armenia. The other fronts were Karakilise (Vanadzor) and Bash Abaran.

anything. Everything is accomplished by force. If we are powerful, then we are able to accomplish our goal.

The Final Journey:

Thinking that this journey is over, there is only one more endeavor left and that one is for the soul. It is our final journey and it is not up to us.

This nation has gone through so many difficulties during the last six hundred years. After going through all these adversities, I was hoping that my children no longer had to go through these hardships themselves.

Praise the Lord that during the final days of my life we have a peaceful and secure existence. Here too I am bothered because in a quarter century my children and grandchildren are going to be lost. I am responsible for this. My heartfelt desire was that my children and I would be born Armenian, would live and die as Armenians and this did not happen. Everything cannot be perfect.

Disappointment and Depression

> Old age should burn and rave at close of day... And
> you, my father, there on the sad height,
> Curse, bless, me now with your fierce tears, I pray.
> Do not go gentle into that good night.
> Rage, rage against the dying of the light.
>
> Dylan Thomas

Some years after immigrating to the U.S., my father became disillusioned and depressed, especially after the assassination of President Kennedy and the Watts Riots of Los Angeles. His depression was aggravated by his loneliness and his difficulty in getting around in the Los Angeles area, since he could not drive. His children were busy with work and family responsibilities. The time for him to interact with family members was mostly limited to weekends and holidays.

In 1966 he decided to take an open ended, long trip by himself and told us that if he liked somewhere else more than America, he may not return. This caused some sleepless nights for all of us, especially for my mother who was left alone at home. He would send occasional postcards from locations he had last been to, with no mention of when he would be returning. He had decided to visit his elderly mother and his brother Parsegh in Beirut. He visited his brother Haig and his family in Armenia. He must have had particular interest in the living conditions in Armenia; but he noted that although life standards had improved since they had immigrated there, the repatriated families still faced limitations due to the Soviet rule. To make a decent living, most of them had to be involved in the black market, in addition to holding onto their regular jobs.

He also went to Istanbul, Turkey, to see his two cousins who were living there. On his way back, he also passed through Europe. Without calling us, one night he arrived in a taxi from LAX. I believe he did not want to admit to us that in spite of all its limitations, America was still the best place to live.

After this sojourn, he spent more time creating relief carvings on wood and marble, mainly a visage of Vartan Mamigonian.
On his trip to Armenia, he had taken one of his carvings to the National Historic Museum in Yerevan. (See Appendix concerning recognition by the National Historic Museum in Yerevan).

POEM: The Days of My Life:

This poem written by my father in the style of epic poems is commonly used in Genocide memoirs.

CHAPTER 11

Etching on Marble of Vartan Mamigonian.

I am Gesaratsi Artin Kitabjian,
Son of Krikor Kitabjian and Arousiag Benlian,
Reign of Turkish king Sultan Hamid in 1895,
Saved from the disastrous massacres.
1896, I was born in Gesaria.
1908, freedom was proclaimed,

LEAVING KAYSERI

This was a game that was played against the Armenians.
1912, I finished elementary school,
For two years I went to the Jesuit school.

Talat and Envar came to power.
In 1914 they gave an order to eliminate the Armenians.
Only Armenians were the deported.
In 1915, August 17, we left the city.

I took the staff in my hand with six people, we started the journey.
I do not know to where.
We got mugged here and there, and we saw days that were unbelievable.
We arrived in the outskirts of Aleppo; they would not let us into the city.
They sent us to Bab, a village.
My father, who was deported to Hama, came and found us in Bab.

We went through illness in the winter,
On the road they mugged and pushed us around.
Meskene, Abu Harara, Sapka. We arrived at Deir el-Zor.
Because we were sick, they would not accept us,
They took us to a place called Marat.
We were healthy but we got sick there.
Out of the 1800 people, only 750 were left after three months.

From Baghdad, we heard the voice of the British.
Turks, being scared,
Distributed us to different villages.
Merciless British were only looking after their own gain. No one asked about the Armenians.

CHAPTER 11

As artisans we stayed in Deir el-Zor.
We lived comfortable days.
We thought about going to Aleppo,
We gathered our belongings,
In ten days we arrived in Aleppo.
Thank God we stayed there for 36 years.
We looked for a more comfortable place.
We said let it be a wise government
That is concerned about the well-being of its people.
We left our property and I left my job,
We started on the road to America.
A few years we were very happy,
However, the stupid people started killing the intelligent ones.[77]
The blacks revolted, and they ruined this place too.
And my thinking got all mixed up,
But the whole world is upside down.
Still we could not find any place better than America.

I often think about our people from the past,
Why were they staying in Turkey, to be massacred?

Wherever you work you will be rewarded.
Find a free country that you will be happy in.
You work hard and enjoy life.
When you have peace of mind you will be able to think,
If you do not make the right decisions
You will not be able to have a family unit.

---

[77] Referring here to the assassinations of both President John F. Kennedy and Rev. Martin Luther King.

We found a free country, and we were very happy.
But freedom (Civil Rights) serves the evil more,
They have taken the freedom away from the
Intelligent people, they rob and kill,
These are the days that we are living in.
I do not think we will see better days after this.
Life in this world is full of pitfalls,
It is not worth to be born to see bad days.
This is it.
To be born and if you do not enjoy life, you will languish.
You are already dead.

Children listen!
Speaking in your native tongue, you are the rose of that nation's bosom. Understand!
But keep your mother tongue unspoiled like a nightingale in roses.
For your nation is the special Ararat among the many mountains, understand that.

Artin Kitabjian

<u>Unforgettable and Hellish Times</u>: Here my father ends his story:

This is a very short account of what I have to say.
Writing everything that has happened would have been impossible, because as I am telling these stories, I get very emotional. I feel like I am going through it all over again. We lived through unforgettable and hellish times.

If I talk about Deir el-Zor for years, there is no end to it. The Armenian people, those who went down that road and managed to stay alive, all have their personal stories.

CHAPTER 11

Here I end my own story. By talking, I get emotional and I become ill.[78]

The Journey

Can't you walk a few more steps?
See the bright sky over those distant hills
To the land of your dreams, always
Seeking safe haven for your family.

Having survived through
The Syrian Desert,
Deir el-Zor killing fields,
You are a survivor,
You can do it.

We will help you.
Take a few more steps.

We are getting closer,
You need to get up
Back on your feet.

Here, drink some water.
A few more steps towards
The land of peace and quiet.

We will carry you
On our shoulders
To the finish line
Of this marathon.

---

[78] Many of the Genocide survivors suffered from Post-Traumatic Stress Disorder associated with depression, re-experiencing the same events and nightmares. Unfortunately the incidence of this phenomenon has not been documented in most of the recorded interviews that we have from the survivors of the Armenian Genocide. There is also evidence that PTSD is manifested in certain number of the progeny of the survivors of the Genocide and it should be further investigated.

LEAVING KAYSERI

Open your eyes, father,
Get up, look, we have reached
The edge of a peaceful ocean.

But my father does not respond!
His eyes are closed and sunken.
A pale, rigid, pulseless corpse.

After almost a century of quest
Looking for safety of his true homeland,
Fatigued, despaired and dispassionate
He has come to rest on the shores of a
Peaceful Ocean.

Having witnessed
Roadside graves,
Tetif, Abu Harrara
On the way to Deir el-Zor,
Aleppo, Beirut,
Apovyan in Armenia,
Andover, Massachusetts, and now
Near the shores of the Pacific,
We have buried dear ones.

Where else on the World map
Will this endless journey take us?
     Gregory Ketabgian, 2010

Letter to My Father

Hearing your voice
Taped over decades

Brings further memories
To the forefront.

Saw your emotion's
Raw edge that last day

CHAPTER 11

In Beirut, while giving
Some advice how to live
One's life away from home.

'Continue your education
Things like marriage can wait'.
For the first time with
Tears in your eyes.

Having survived the road to Deir el-Zor
While losing your sister and brother,
Now wanted to hold onto family,
Children for allowed infinity.

Giving up your secure income,
To follow them, foreign lands
With unknown risks and languages
To remain true to ideals.

Your prophetic predictions
Have come true
As you saw them.

To satisfy curiosity
To convey your story
To our grandchildren
In deliberate fashion
To avoid apprehension.

Greater challenges
Face us today,
Everything does not work out as desired;
"To be born, live and die as an Armenian."

We are in need of sage advice,
Your loving son.
      Gegory Ketabgian, 2008

LEAVING KAYSERI

Ending

All stories eventually have to have an ending. Most of the time we like to have stories that reach a pleasant conclusion. However as life itself, how it all will end is not under our control. As a writer once said, "Our lives do not reach a dramatic climax in the way that books usually do. Most of us just go on day to day through major and minor trials and defeats. And finally time runs out."[79] Of course the interpretation of an ending will be up to each individual. I have read many life stories of individuals, biographies and recently obituaries, where it is considered a good ending when one has been successful in life, when one has reached an executive position, made millions in business or when his or her name has frequently appeared in society columns.

But will that be considered a "good story," a success? Whatever they may have accomplished, did it affect other people's lives as well as the lives of their family members? These matters are of paramount importance during the uncertain times and the complex environment in which we are living and our children and grandchildren are growing up. These considerations will influence the direction the next generations will likely take.

Our fathers thought that by getting their families and children out of harm's way into safety would give us a chance to live a full life of pleasant experiences. They were right in getting us out of the countries with unstable governments, but they could not foresee the dangers that lurked in the present day society in the U.S. The rising crime rate and the decay of moral fiber in these times, as my father mentions in his advice to us, are major concerns in raising a family in these challenging times.

---

[79] Conolly Jr. Evan S. LA Times, Jan. 11, 2013. P. AA6

In addition, trying to preserve some small segment of the Armenian culture and language among future generations is a major task and at this time it seems we already are losing the battle.

Having said all of the above, we still have to have hope for the future because that is the only way to survive. In my experience, having come across a large number of individuals facing very difficult life situations, I have observed that those who have the fighting spirit do much better and survive in spite of all the disasters they have had to face. Furthermore, I think the ones who survived the deportations, disease, starvation and killings were the ones that did not give up and kept at it and by some unbelievable turn of events, persisted until the whole calamity ran out of energy and came to an end. We have to get this message across to the future generations and energize them as much as we can that our story is not a story of failure to be depressed about, but a story of success and survival against all odds.

Some of the statements in the recent past from our grandchildren have made us more hopeful that what we are trying to accomplish will most likely survive for the foreseeable future.

Trans-generational life is a work in progress. We do not have the right to interrupt that process by being pessimistic. We have to get the message across to our children and to our children's children that a strong sense of "intergenerational self-image," that they belong to something bigger than themselves, will help create a greater sense of self-esteem within them.

I have friends, who after being told what our grandchildren have stated, have suggested that I include those utterances as a reason to be positive for the future. They said it could serve as a good ending to this long but incomplete story, **a journey of one hundred years.** So here they are:

LEAVING KAYSERI

The first comment was related to us by Beatrice's[80] Latino baby sitter, who had taken her to their local congressman's office when she was seven, to object to the passage of stricter laws against immigrants. After everyone was finished with their statements, the congressman had asked if there were any further comments. Beatrice had raised her hand and made the following statement: "My Grandparents are Armenian immigrants who had come here many years ago and their parents had walked in the desert without water and food to survive. Therefore we have to be good to the immigrants in this country. I also want to tell you a short story that my grandfather has told me," and she told them the anecdote of the Golden Bracelet.

Next comment was by Noah. This occurred about four years ago at age six while we were locating different countries on the globe and discussing longitudes and latitudes. The conversation turned to the Sahara desert. As I was describing that it was the largest desert and so on, Noah wanted to know, "Where is the desert that your father had walked through without water and food?" It took a few moments for me to recover from the unexpected question, since I did not remember mentioning these issues to him at any time in the past.

The next statement was from Lydia age 5 who had written short sentences for Christmas in her class for members of our family. The card for Grandmother Alice stated, "I cherish my grandmother because some kids do not have any."

My wife and I feel fortunate to be the children of survivors who miraculously persevered against amazing odds and after hard work and enormous effort, got us out of the countries which had undependable and unfriendly governments towards their minority citizens. Recent political upheavals threatening the safety of the

---

[80] The oldest one of our grandchildren, Beatrice Hannah Youd; the others being Noah Artin Math and Lydia Fay Math.

ENDING

Armenians and other Christian populations both in Syria, Iraq, Egypt and Turkey emphasize the importance of these statements.

The Old Oak Tree

"We need to see the oak tree with the fungus"
Says Noah Artin.
The old oak tree, only a shell of its old self,
Emptied out to the top
Where the honey-golden fungus
Still present
To do its malignant destruction
Like cancer.

Old oak tree ready to fall with the next storm,
As old grandfathers do.

But wait! This one has green leaves on its branches,
Ample acorns to keep squirrels happy for another season.

Powerful branches leaning on a much younger one
Naturally grafted, supporting and nourishing,
Stronger than a crutch, undying for now,
Older generation supported by the vibrant youth.

Youth weighed down with the weight of
Grave memories of the past generations.
Stronger, enjoying from the contact and
Blessing of the grandparents. [81]

Gregory Ketabgian 2010

---

[81] The old oak tree was actually present at a Calabasas park with a manmade lake close to where Noah's parents lived at that time and we used to take walks every Friday after picking them up from preschool.

APPENDICES

Advice to My Nation

There is no end to this writing. We came to America and have lived some good days, but now within the last ten years, it is changing progressively, deteriorating by all the killings and robberies. Besides, people are after bodily pleasures and drinking. Do not laugh. Do not blame me. They are after obscene games and demonstrations. They are competing to expose their body parts and become more pornographic.

This world is a dream, a beautiful life and an invisible power. The world's scientists are working to find new secrets and by pure chance a lot of new treatments are being discovered. The world is full of secrets. We need intelligent people and time to accomplish this. While some of the people are working on progress, others are working on regression. Still others are working on obscenity, but it will not go unpunished. In pursuing bodily pleasures they are risking their health, shortening their life and even risking death.

People with average intelligence can live well if they do not get involved with risky activities. The family can be educated by sending their offspring to school. The ones with additional wealth can benefit their nation and leave a good reputation for themselves.

Is there anyone thinking serious matters or do they want to enjoy today only with bodily pleasures?

The ones born to this garden are all brothers and sisters. But they have become enemies due to greed and religion. And they devour each other. Have you seen other living four footed animals like us? They do not devour their kind. We call them animals, but their brains do not work like ours. They do not think about war. And they do not think about damaging their type. They do not know how to write and read but they do not kill their nation's children. Why have wars?

Within the last 100 years I have seen lots of progress in the standard of living. People have benefitted from these; however, they are not aware of its value and continue to kill each other. I have been a fortunate person. We saw bad days; we went to Deir el-Zors. Some of us miraculously survived and came all the way to Los Angeles. The year is 1978 and I am 82 years old. We are happy as a family. Unless you have seen hellish days, you do not know the value of the peaceful days. As it is, life is full of difficulties. Among all these guns and this much enmity, it is impossible to find peace. Why should we be enemies? The reason is monetary gain.

I give thanks to all these amazing creations that I have come across in my days. I enjoyed and lived the life given to me, which happens to very few. For eighty two years I enjoyed life with my family in the gardens of this world, we had a good life.

A thousand thanks to the Creator.

As this world turns and the days pass, do not wait to enjoy it, do it today. Do not waste your time, the day does not seek you; do not let the day go by. Give thanks to the Creator until you finish your travels.

Before you take on a task, ask yourself and your conscience how to approach it correctly. This will prevent you from facing obstacles. So that you will not have to ask for forgiveness or have to constantly say, "I am sorry." Do you understand? Pay attention to your problems. By praying one thousand times to be pardoned is inconsequential and it is a lie, do not believe it. You would have fooled yourself. You cannot pay your debt with prayer. It is obvious all nations are enemies of each other. It is my idea that religions are the cause. All nations want others to worship to the same religion that they believe in. They are convinced that their religion is the real one. All the religions are the same. They are all worshipping the same Creator. It is similar to all the rivers that eventually flow into the sea. They are using religion as an excuse to make war and profit from it. But no one thinks about the young ones; come and ask the fathers and the mothers. The heads of governments are pitiless and nonreligious people. They wipe out millions of lives with a single word. It is impossible to mend this enmity in the future. Instead it will get worse in time. What they had said was right, the world has behaved this way and will not change. Do not spend *your time trying to figure it out, because there is no logical explanation. The wealthy countries have millions and they want to amass billions. But there is no place for them to take in the end, they were dust and they will turn to dust. Only think about your livelihood, so that you can live your life fully.*

Kitabjian Family Genealogy (Partial)

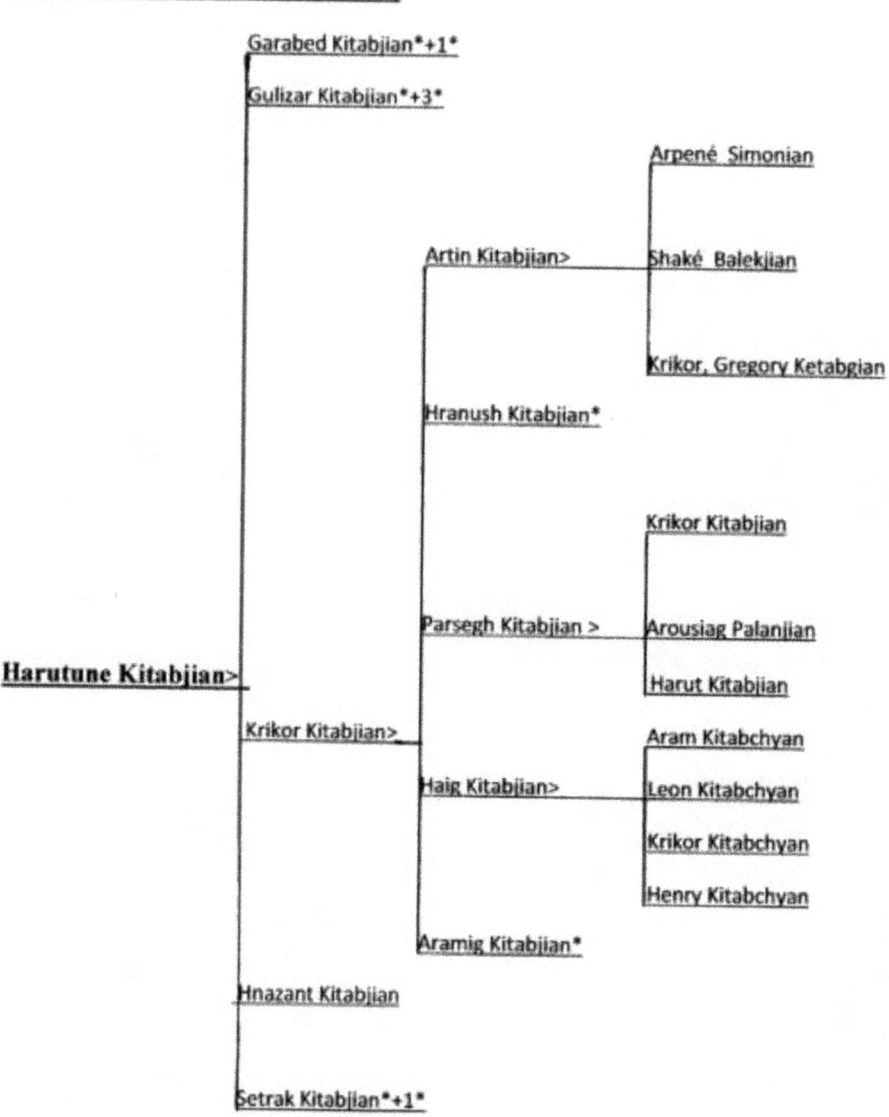

* (Asterisks indicate those who died during 1915, for a total of 10 members.)

Matossian Family Genealogy (Partial)

- **Sarkis Matossian>**
  - Yacoub Matossian>
    - Behia Tejirian> — Mary Krecky
    - Vahide Dekmejian> — Hrair Dekmejian
    - Mary Kassabian
    - Rahel Khachaturian> — Zaven Khachaturian
    - Arous Samuelian
    - Beatrice Kitabjian>
      - Arpené Simonian
      - Shaké Balekjian
      - Krikor Ketabgian
    - Hagop Matossian>
      - Raffi Matossian
      - Tina Assadourian
      - Jesse Matossian
    - Sarkis Matossian>
      - Sarkis Matossian Jr.
      - Annette Matossian
      - Alex Matossian
    - Nerses Matossian>
      - Karen Matossian
      - Cathy Matossian
  - Toros Matossian
  - Lucia Matossian
  - Movses Matossian
  - Jesse Matossian*

*(Asterisk indicates those who died during 1915)

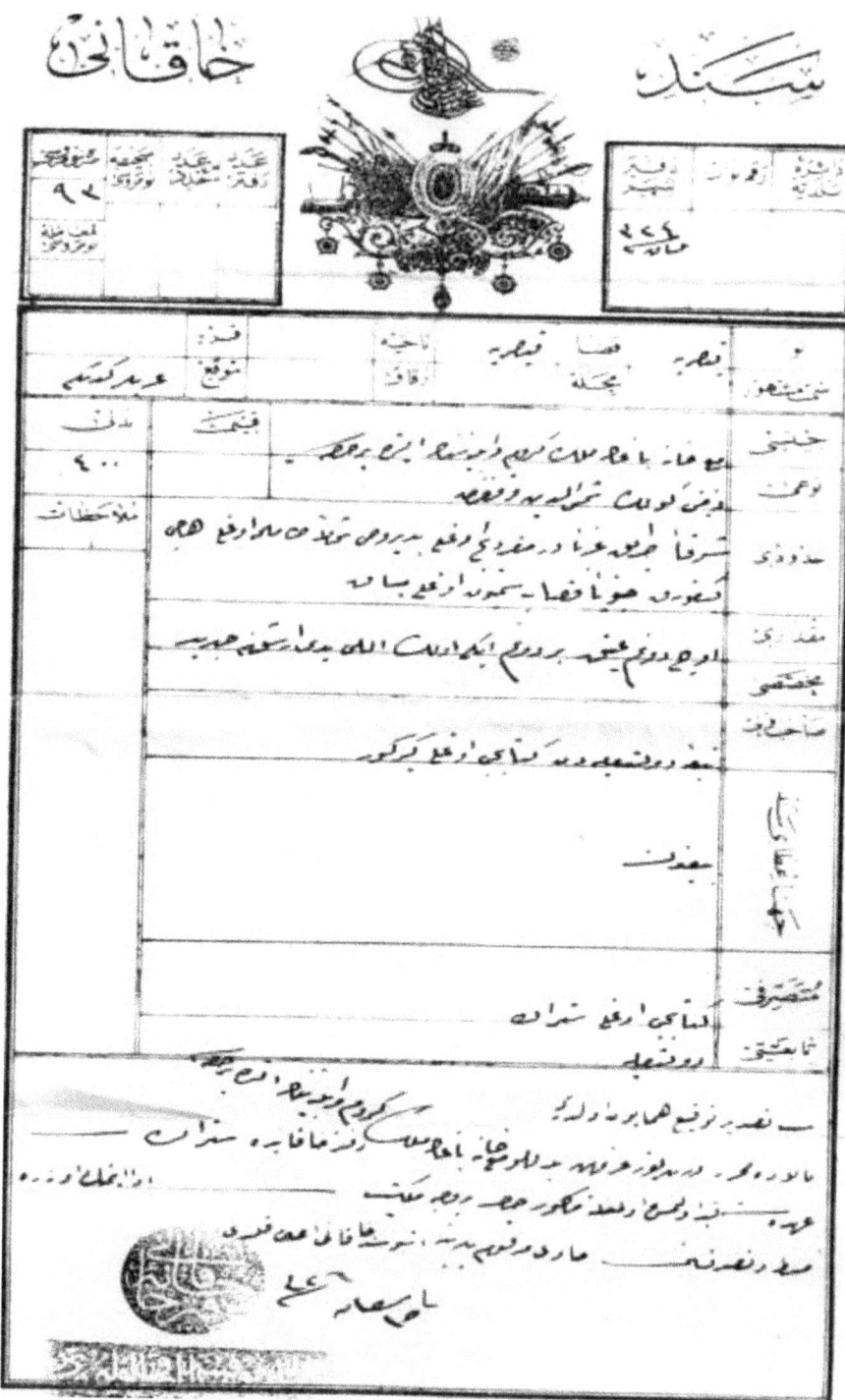

APPENDICES

SENED-Ý HÂKÂNÎ

Defter-i þehr: Nisan 324
Sýra numarasý (number of series): 96

Liva (equivalent to province): Kayseriyye
Arablar Gidiðine

Kaza (district): Kayseriyye

Cinsi (type, category): Ma-hane bað yerinin altýda iki hissesi [two portion-share below Mahane]

Nev'i: Evkâfa mülhak Gölek Þemseddin Vakfý müþtemilâtýndan [annexes-outbuildings t Semseddin Foundation]

Hududu [boundaries –of the property]: Þarkan tarîk garben Der Mýgýrdýç oðlu Bedirc Tamîlha oðlu Hâci Kigork cenûben Kasap Simon oðlu Misak

Miktarý [amount- how big]: Üç dönüm atîk bir dönüm iki evlek elli yedi arþýn-ý cedîd [c dönüm=a land measure of 1000 square meters (about a quarter of an acre).]

Cihet-i ita-yý sened [date of the voucher given]: Nisan 317 tarihli senedinin tebdilinde

Mutasarrýfý [owner]: Kitapçý oðlu Terak

Tabiiyeti [citizenship]: Devlet-i âliye

Sebeb-i tastîr-i tevkî'-i hümâyûn oldur ki
Bâlâda muharrer ma-hane bað yerinin altýda iki hissesi defter-i hâkânîde Terak uhdesin olmaðla hane yerinin iki buçuk guruþlu mukataasýyla bað yerinin a'þâr-ý þer'iyesir etmek üzere zabt ve tasdîkini havi merkum yedinde iþbu sene-i hâkânî i'tâ kýlýndý
[Here it explains why this document is given; what I understand is that the person who s gives to the new owner a voucher [bond-bill] –we don't know the reason- and since this i related to house and land state takes its own taxes]

(mühür)

One of the house deeds from Kayseri for Kitabchioglu Terak (Setrak) that was translated by Taner Akcam.

LEAVING KAYSERI

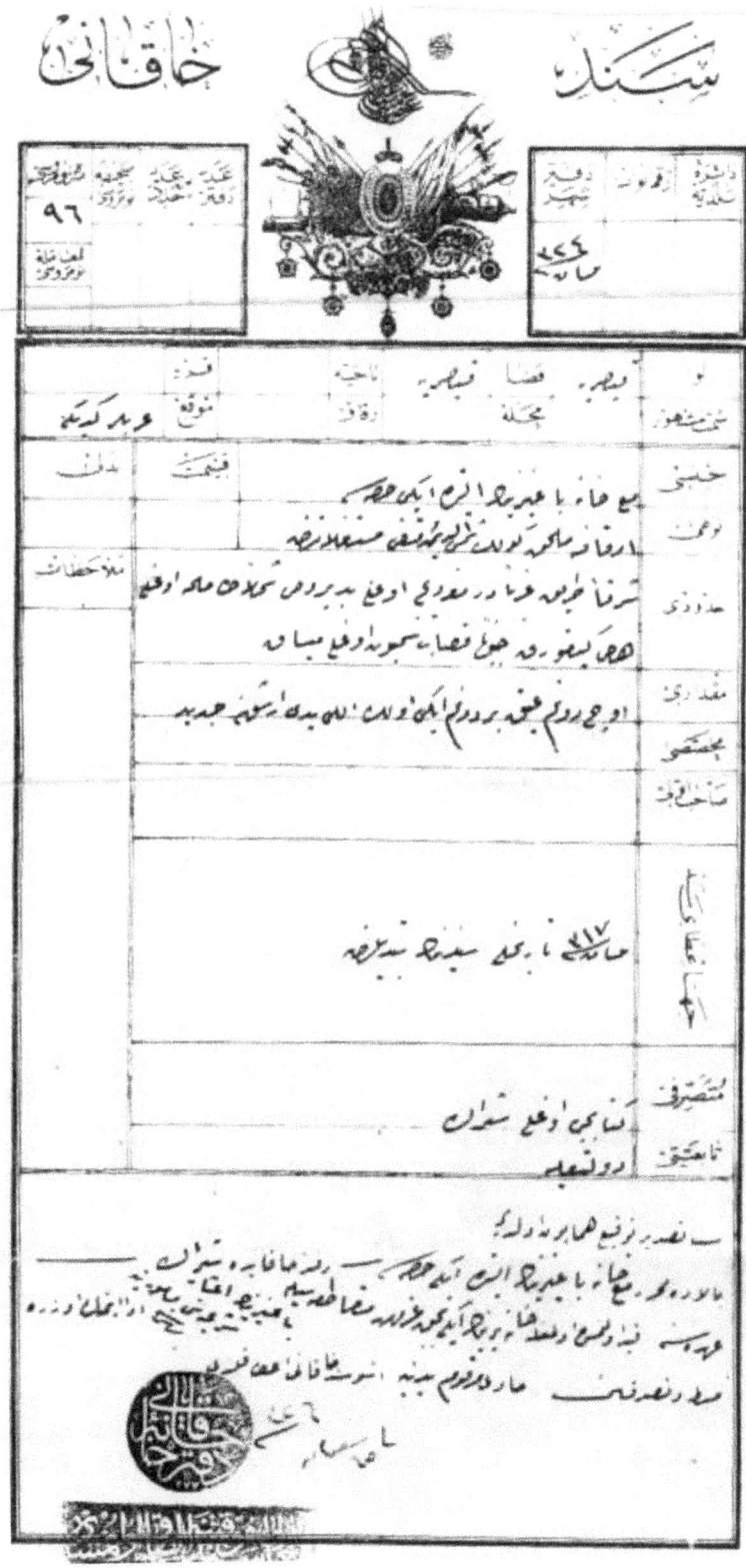

APPENDICES

Top: Military ID sent with orders for hard labor imprisonment. Bottom: My Syrian passport with the change in the spelling of my name.

LEAVING KAYSERI

Excambion, our ship's schedule and ports of call, the last line underlined.

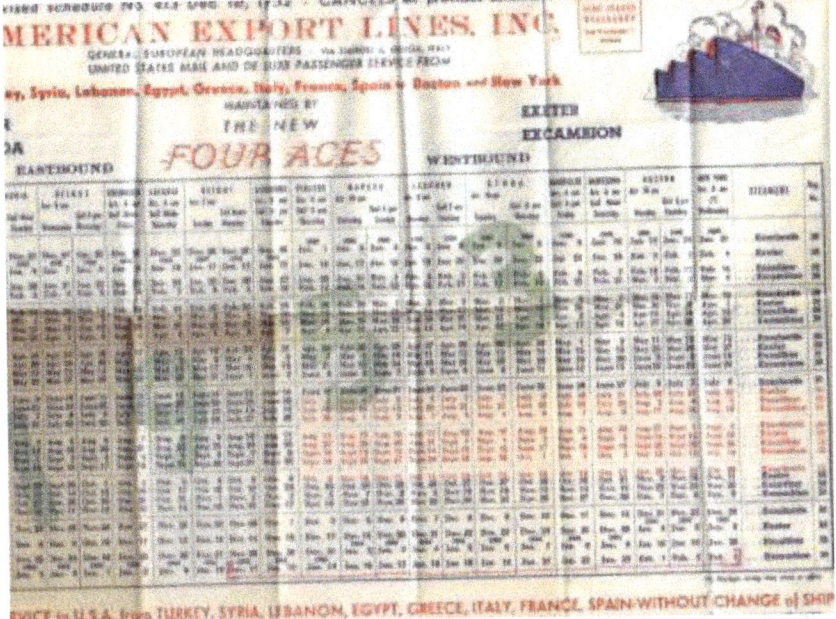

APPENDICES

Syrian ID card and inside of Syrian Passport.

LEAVING KAYSERI

In a publication of the National Cultural Museum, acknowledgment and pictures of the donations of my father's etchings and an embroidered silk table cover and other needle point works of my mother.

APPENDICES

ՀԱՅԿԱԿԱՆ ՍՈՎԵՏԱԿԱՆ ՍՈՑԻԱԼԻՍՏԱԿԱՆ ՌԵՍՊՈՒԲԼԻԿԱՅԻ ԳԻՏՈՒԹՅՈՒՆՆԵՐԻ ԱԿԱԴԵՄԻԱ
АКАДЕМИЯ НАУК АРМЯНСКОЙ СОВЕТСКОЙ СОЦИАЛИСТИЧЕСКОЙ РЕСПУБЛИКИ

ՊԵՏԱԿԱՆ ՊԱՏՄԱԿԱՆ ԹԱՆԳԱՐԱՆ   ГОСУДАРСТВЕННЫЙ ИСТОРИЧЕСКИЙ МУЗЕЙ

ՇՆՈՐՀԱԿԱԼԱԳԻՐ

[Letter text in Armenian handwriting]

ԴԻՐԵԿՏՈՐ ՊԱՏՄՈՒԹՅԱՆ   Կ. ՄԵԼԻՔՍԵԹՅԱՆ

ԱՇԽԱՏԱՆՑ ԲԱԺՆԻ ՎԱՐԻՉ   Կ. ԱՐԱՔՍՄԱՆՑԻ

Above two receipts from the National Cultural Museum of Yerevan, Armenia for the donation given them on June 28, 1966 by both of my parents of their handiwork representing their origins from Antep and Kayseri, Turkey.

APPENDICES

Gesaratsi Stories

There are a number of anecdotal accounts of Gesaratsis that have been told through the years, mostly to emphasize their pride and success as well as to teach the younger generations about their way of life. It was important to train their children to prepare them for survival in the competitive world outside. Gesaratsis are mainly thought to be extremely frugal and calculating in their daily activities, although it also highlights the dangers of being extra-frugal. They felt proud to be a Gesaratsi and I remember my father would seek out other survivors from his city during Armenian Church picnics in California. Once he found one, they would have an immediate bonding. (**Warning to readers**: this section contains some improper ethnic, religious and graphic material).

The Painted Donkey. The Gesaratsi paints his donkey black before taking it to the donkey bazaar to sell it. Apparently, a black donkey was more valuable than a gray or brown one. He sells it to a non-suspecting customer from another village. The new owner, while on his way home, notes the paint getting washed off from the rain. The villager says, "Too bad, the Gesaratsi outwitted me again."

I read about a recent variation of this story in a travel book about Turkey, where the son of a Turk from Kayseri paints his mother and sells her to his father for a second wife. Enough said.

How to Light a Cigarette. This is a story of a young man who had convinced his wealthy old uncle to finance his new business venture. At the end of the transaction after the old man gives him the money, the young man thanks him and lights a cigarette with his match to celebrate. The old uncle demands the money back since he was not frugal enough. He tells him that he should have used a cinder from the fireplace instead of wasting a match.

Gesaratsi's Horse. Trying to cut down his overhead cost on his farm, the Gesaratsi decides to gradually cut down on the amount of feed for his dependable horse. The horse starts losing weight and one day falls over and dies. "Too bad," says the Gesaratsi, "I had just about trained him to get along on no food."

Patriarch of the Family. The Patriarch of the family was on his death bed. The elder son approached the bed slowly asking him for any last words and pearls on how to manage the family without him. He said, "Listen, you know the cow we have in the barn. Slaughter him." But the son says that they depend on that cow for their milk, butter and yoghurt. He says, "I know that, but listen, you make basterma from the meat, but take the intestines and after cleaning them well, throw them into our well. That way you will have ample "*patcha*" soup for generations to come."

Gesaratsi's Basterma. Gesaratsis took great pride in their preparation of *Basterma*. But more than the preparation, they took great pride in slicing it thin and evenly. The well-known Bastermagis in Istanbul and Aleppo were of course Armenians from Gesaria. Next episode brings out the important role *Basterma* played in their lives in an extreme fashion.

An Armenian gentleman in Istanbul was waiting in the long line to get on the ferry to cross the Bosphorus when he met a rich Turkish friend of his who asked him why he was taking the ferry. He said he had to deliver a package to his brother on the Asian side. His friend, the Turk offered to take the package for him.
When they got on the ferry, the Turk gave the package to his helper to carry. The helper went outside to sit on the deck. Because the package smelled interesting, he opened one end and tasted the *basterma* within.

When they got off the ferry, they met the other brother, who inquired about the package. The Turk asked the helper for it, who after some hesitation admitted that he ate it all. The Armenian brother attacked the helper and was ready to strangle him if bystanders had not interfered. The Turk wanted to know what could be in the package that was so valuable, and was willing to replace it. After the brother settled down, he admitted that his mother had recently passed away in Syria; her last wish was to be buried in her birthplace in Gesaria, Turkey. Since the Turkish government would not allow such a burial, they had thought of this ingenious idea of the Basterma. It was finally decided that the helper could only redeem his act by working for the Armenian brothers for the remainder of his life. In addition, when he passed away, he was to be buried in their mother's plot. (I am indebted for this story to Leo Hamalian, the previous editor of the now defunct Ararat Journal published by AGBU.)

The Armenian Priest On a lighter note, my father used to tell two short anecdotal stories about priests: The first one takes place on a boat while crossing a river. The priest falls into the river. The occupants all stretch their arms and ask the priest to give his hand so that they can pull him back into the boat. But the priest somehow is reluctant to do so. One of the helpers realizes the situation and recommends them to say, "Father, take my hand," instead of what they had been saying, "Father, give your hand." This is because the priest would only take offerings.

The second story has to do with a priest's beard. After church while people were socializing in the church yard, one of the parishioners asks the priest whether he sleeps with his beard under the covers or outside. The priest becomes perplexed, but after thinking about it says that he does not remember. However on that night and for a number of nights subsequently, he has difficulty in sleeping since he wonders where to place his beard. Eventually he shaves it off...

The Money Can (Tenekeh) The people of a town were celebrating the victory of a younger candidate with a parade because he was replacing an older incumbent, a long term mayor. The older mayor (*Mukhtar*) seeing their elation calls them over and tells them, "Stupid people, you don't know what you have just done. My money-can (*Tenekeh*) needed only four more finger widths to be filled up to the top. Now, this new guy has to start from the bottom." Tenekeh was a four gallon tin can that they would fill with gold pieces, the usual safe currency of the time. (I am indebted to my sister, Shaké Balekjian for having remembered my father telling this anecdote about graft, a common practice there.)

Gesaratsi college student (Another one from my sister, Shaké)
The Gesaratsi student in a college class was sitting in the back row when the teacher wanted to give them different examples about being frugal (was he also Gesaratsi?) and saving energy at the same time. He asked the person closest to the light switch to turn off the lights during his lecture, since there were no visual presentations. At the end of the lecture, the teacher asked him to turn on the lights. The Gesaratsi student asked to delay turning on the lights for a minute. When the lights came on, the teacher asked him what the reason for the delay was. The Gesaratsi admitted that he had taken off his pants so that they would not wear out.

Beshi-Birlik Gold Piece.
A Jewish merchant, noticing there were no competitors in an Armenian town and planning to settle there, notices a five year old child playing with *Beshi-Birlik* Gold piece (Gold coin worth five gold pieces). He offers the child 5 to 6 bright copper coins instead of his coin piece. The child answers him saying, "Without taking your copper coins I will give my shiny coin piece if you can bray three times like a donkey." The merchant looks around to make sure no one is nearby and brays like a donkey. When he asks for the gold coin, the child answers, "Hey you Donkey, if as a donkey you were able to notice that my coin was gold, wouldn't I, being human, know that the other coins you showed me were copper?" The merchant continues on his journey.

Another Merchant Story.
Another merchant looking to settle in a town, notices some youngsters playing a game called "Guess what I am thinking." He approaches them and asks them what kind of profitable business there was in their town. One of the boys asks for a dime for each one of them to give him the answer. After being paid he tells him, "Here in Kayseri they make a lot of *Basterma* from the meat of the cow. After they slaughter the animal, they throw away the intestine and the tripe. If you are a capable person and collect the intestines, you eat the inside contents to satisfy your hunger and

sell the tripe to make a profit." When the merchant hears this, he realizes he cannot make a living in that town. (Alboyajian, p. 699-700)

The Black Bras. Another recent story has to do with the Gesaratsi who had immigrated to Brooklyn, New York and had opened a store next to a Jewish clothier. The Jewish storekeeper had previously gotten a good rate on a large shipment of black bras; however, they were not popular and they did not sell. His Gesaratsi neighbor offers to take them off his hands real cheap. The Gesaratsi cuts the straps off and displays them as yarmulkes!

GLOSSARY

A

Agha: Lord or Master.

Aintab or Antep: Now called Gaziantep by the Turks, a city on the southeastern part of the country close to the Syrian border. Residents are called Aintabtsis.

Aleppo: a city on the north western part of Syria also called *Haleb* by its inhabitants.

Ana: Grandmother.

Anatolia: Also called Asia Minor, the peninsular landmass on which present day Turkey is situated.

Arak: Raki, common liquor in the Middle-East. Anise flavored alcohol.

Avedic Isahakian: Armenian poet considered the bard of Armenian folk poems. (1875-1957)

B

Badarak: Mass

Baklava: A dessert made with multiple layers of thin dough with the center with walnuts and cinnamon.

Basterma: cured, spicy meat.

Bey: Title inferior to Pasha but superior to Agha.

Boereg: Cheese in a pocket of dough. Varieties with meat, onions, spinach stuffing and the dough being baklava paper thin type.

Bozanti: A pass through the Tauros Mountains.

Bulghur: Cracked wheat.

Burma: A dessert with its center packed with pistachios surrounded with a browned layer of kadaef dough.

Bustan Keleb: (Garden of Dogs) Commercial section of Aleppo.

Bzdig: Small or young.

C

Caravan: a train of pack animals (camels).

Chavoush: Sargent.

Chettes: Band of brigands.

Chechen: Circassian Muslim race living along the Caucauses.

Chezok: Neutral, not affiliated with any party.

Cilicia: Giligia in Armenian. Southeastern portion of Turkey bound by the Mediterranean Sea in the south and Taurus

GLOSSARY

Mountains in the north. Name changed to Chukhurova by the Turks.

Constantinople: Old historic name of Istanbul named by Emperor Constantine of Eastern Roman Empire (Constantinopolis, Bolis by its Armenian residents).

D

Dashnak: a member of Dashnatsutyun (Armenian Revolutionary Federation, ARF) political party founded in 1890 as an Armenian left wing organization to fight against Ottoman injustices.

Deir el-Zor: a town in eastern Syrian Desert on the Euphrates River. Most of the survivors of the deportation during the Genocide of 1915 were killed in the vicinity of this town.

Dolma: Vegetables that are stuffed with usually a mixture of ground meat and rice or bulgur. The most common vegetables are eggplant, zucchini, peppers and tomatoes.

E

Elia Kazan: (Kazangioglu) Author, playwright, movie producer of Greek descent whose father and uncle were immigrants from Kayseri.

Erciyes: Mountain near Kayseri (Archeos or Argaeus).
Erevan: Capital of Republic of Armenia also Yerevan.
Erysipelas: An infection of the soft tissue of skin by streptococcus bacteria.

F

G

Gamichly: Fertile farming region of the extreme northeastern section of Syria. Also spelled Quamichli.

Gendarme: Policeman.

Gesaria: name given to the town of Kayseri by Armenians (from the original Roman name of Cesaria). A Gesaratsi is a person from that town. Gesaratsis are the Armenian inhabitants and descendants of those individuals.

Ghatmer: A layered pastry with butter like a croissant.
Giligia: see Cilicia as referred to by Armenians.
Golgotha: A difficult uphill journey, compared to Christ carrying his cross up the Golgotha Mountain.

Groong: Crane.

H

Hammal: Porter.

Hammos or Hummus: Ground chick peas mixed with sesame seed oil and garlic and lemon juice.

Harissa: Cooked smashed or hurled wheat that is cooked mashed and mixed with meat or chicken.

Hunchak: a member of Hunchakian (Social Democratic Hunchakian Party) was founded 1887 to liberate Armenians from Ottoman rule.

I

Ittihad ve Terrakki: political party in power during WWI in Turkey also called Committee of Union and Progress or CUP for short.

J

Jihad: a holy war waged on behalf of Islam as a religious duty, usually proclaimed and sanctioned by the supreme religious leader.

K

Kaghge: Pastry made out of flour with egg wash and sesame seeds on top.

Karabagh: Region historically inhabited by Armenians that was liberated after the breakup of Soviet Union, also referred to as Nagorno-Karabagh and Artsakh by its Armenian inhabitants.

Karasoon Manuk: Forty Brave Youth, during early Christianity a Roman captain knowing that some of his troops had converted to Christianity, forced them to enter a freezing lake near Sivas to see how strong their faith was. Karasoon Mangants is the church dedicated to their memory.

Kaymakam: Governor of a region.

Kayseri: City in middle of Anatolia, present day Turkey. "Gesaria" in Armenian.

Kemancha: A small string musical instrument with a bulbous belly played upright resting on one's knee with a sweet tone and good ability for vibrato.

Kete or Kata: Pastry with a center of khorez, which is flour in butter with innovative designs on the surface of the piece.

Khachkar: Cross Stones. Sculpted from Tufa stone, relief of

cross figures with different carved details.

Khoong: Incense.

Korzitch: Party worker.

Kufta: Many varieties of ground meat mixed with cracked wheat, bulgur, made into oblong egg shaped pieces. Other varieties include flat in a pan, smaller ones with butter in the center in a yoghurt broth or others made with lentil without meat for Lent.

Kurd: A member of pastoral and agriculture people of Islamic faith living in Eastern Anatolia as well as northern Iraq and Syria.

L

Lahmajoun: also called "Armenian Pizza", spicy mixture of ground meat and vegetables on thin flattened dough cooked fairly crisp in the bakery oven. The name is Arabic meaning meat on bread.

Lusavorchagan: The Illuminator, named after St. Gregory the Illuminator, who established the Christian church in Armenia in 301 AD as the official church of the nation.

M

Mangal: Brasier.

Manti: Spicy meat placed in flat dough similar to a ravioli but in the shape of a butterfly, eaten usually in a broth with tomato paste and sumac.

Mesrobian letters: The Armenian alphabet that was discovered by a monk, Mesrob Mashdots.

Metz: Older or big.

Mezza: Middle–Eastern hors d'oeuvres.

Muhajeer: Refugee

Mujettera: A form of pilav with lentils and either wheat or rice.

Muslim: people who adhere to Islamic faith. "Moslem" used as a variation.

N

Nahadag: Martyr

Nerkacht: Repatriation usually referred to Armenians emigrating to Soviet Armenia.

Nufus Kaghidi: Identification paper.

O

P

Patcha: A thick broth soup usually made by boiling the bones of lamb's (pig's) feet, eaten with bread crumbs and lots of garlic.

Pasha: Highest title for Turkish military or civil officials.

Q

R

Raki: see Arak above.

Ramazan: Islamic holy days of fasting during the daylight hours and feasting after sundown.

S

Saint Gregory the Illuminator: Soorp Krikor Lusavoritch, the priest responsible for Armenia becoming the first Christian nation.

Sarma: Wrapped grape leaves stuffed with dolma mixtures or just rice with onions, spicing, raisins and walnuts and called false, meaning without meat.

Sebil: A public fountain.

Sevkiat: Deportation or deportee.

Sultan Hamid: the infamous sultan of Turkey who was also known as the "Red Sultan" because he had ordered repeated massacres of Armenians throughout his reign.

T

Talas: A mountainous suburb of Kayseri.

Tomarza: A small town east of Kayseri.

U

V

Vartan Mamigonian: The commander of the Armenians forces that fought and lost against a much superior Persian army to defend their faith in Christianity in 451 AD.

W

X

Y

Yavrous: "My child" or "my son".

Yerevan: Capital of Republic of Armenia also Erevan.

Z

Zeytoon: A town in the northern mountains of Cilicia known for its independent spirit. Zeytoontsy is a resident or a descendent of one from Zeytoun (alternate spelling).

Pictures and Maps Acknowledgments

GK= Gregory Ketabgian photographer.
AK= Artin Kitabjian phototgrapher.

Genocide Map. Page 4. Permission ANI.
Chapter 1
Kitabjian Family Portrait, 1909. Photographkaniye Ergias, Timourian and Mostichian.
Ercyas Mountain. GK
Picture of the prisoners by Gulbenk (Chichekian) supplied by Steven Kurkjian.

Chapter 2
Large Fountain. GK
St. Gregory the Illuminator Church. GK
Altar of St. Gregory Church. GK
Genocide Map. Permission for use from ANI obtained (on file).

Chapter 3
Sebil-Garden. AK
Sebil with bike. AK
Arous Ana. Unkn.
Bitias Church courtyard. Photographer unknown.
Abughalghal bus. AK
Abughalghal water site and father's camera and case. AK

Chapter 4
Arous Ana. Aleppo, 1928. Photographer unknown.
Krikor Kitabjian. Aleppo, 1928. Photographer unknown.
Pocket knife. GK

Chapter 5
Aleppo Postcard. V. Derounian, Alep, Syrie. 1924
Extended Kitabjian family. Aleppo. 1920. Photographer unknown.

Chapter 6
Wedding Picture, September 21, 1925. Photographer Agop, Aleppo.

ACKNOWLEDGEMENTS

Chapter 7
Shira large pot & Boiling the juice. AK Picnic in Lebanese apple orchard. AK

Chapter 8
Ramadanieh gas station. GK
Kitabjian cousins in Aleppo. AK

Chapter 9
Kitabjian Family Portrait 1950, Aleppo, Syria. Photo Diana, Alep.

Chapter 11
Etching on marble of Vartan Mamigonian by Artin Kitabjian. GK

Bibliography

Alboyajian, Arshag A. *The History of Armenian Gesaria*. Cairo, Egypt: Hagop Papazian Press, 1937, 2 volumes (in Armenian).

Badmakrian, A & Missirlian, E. *Tankaran Haygagan Erkeru*. Vosgedar Printing, 1940, Cairo, Egypt (In Armenian).

Conolly Jr. Evans, *LA Times*, Jan 11, 2013. p. AA6

Dadrian, Vahakn "The Agency of "Triggering Mechanisms" as a Factor in the Organization of the Genocide against the Armenians of Kayseri District." *Genocide Studies and Prevention* 1, 2 (September 2006).

Derderian, Mae. *Vergeen: A Survivor of the Armenian Genocide*. Los Angeles; Atmus Press Publication, 1966.

Kaghtsrouni, Arshavir, *"Corpse Covered Field", Artsakang*, Gesaria Charitable Union 1963. Beirut, Lebanon. (Armenian) Translated by Gregory Ketabgian.

Kazan, Elia. *The Arrangement*. Stein and Day, 1967.
Kazan, Elia. *America, America*. Popular Library, 1964.

Kevorkian, Raymond, *The Armenian Genocide. A Complete History,* I.B.Taurus, London, New York, 2011.

Koundakjian, Armine Carapetian *The Repression of Armenian Repatriates During the Stalin Era*. Yerevan, 2012. (Self-published).

Kurkjian, Steven NAASR lecture; "Kiss My Children's Eyes", personal communication. Sept. 2006.

BIBLIOGRAPHY

Armenian Weekly, April 22, 2014 (Detailed article with identification of most of the individuals in front of the jail.

Hai Antep, The Union of Armenians of Antep Inc. Vol VI 1965, No. 3 (Edited by Krikor Bogharian, my elementary principal at Gertasiratz, in Aleppo, Syria)

Odian, Yervant. *Cursed Years, 1914-1919,* Nairi, Yerevan, 2004. (In Aremenian)

Phillips, Terry, "*Murder at the Altar*". Hye Books, Bakersfield, CA 2008.

Realizing a Dream, Then and Now, AGBU Magazine, Vol. 20, Nov. 2010.

Sarkissian, Khacher, *My Memoires of Seventy Years,* G. Donikian & Fils, Beirut, Lebanon. (in Armenian) 1970.

Sheridan, James: *Chinese Warlord: Career of Feng Yu-hsiang.* Stanford Unive. Press, 1966.

Yapoujian, Hagazoun, "*Rumdigin Memoirs"* Dbaran Atlas, Beyrout, 1967. (In Armenian)

Acknowledgments

First and foremost I again want to thank my sister Shaké Balekjian and her husband Garbis and son Gary for translating my father's tapes into English.

Next I want to thank our good friend and mentor, Gail Tager, who read one of the early forms of the manuscript with critical suggestions to improve the understanding of the journey by a non-Armenian.

Most valuable was the reading by Dr. Richard H. Dekmejian. When asked to look at it for historical accuracy, he instead went through it with a fine toothcomb correcting punctuation and spelling in addition to other constructive criticism.

I need to mention here the relentless interest and enthusiasm of Maggie Mangasarian Gochin, the director of the Ararat Eskijian Museum at Misson Hills, who would constantly be on the lookout for additional resource material and interest in the progression of the book. In addition I want to thank the following for their suggestion: Judy Tanielian, Dr. Donald Miller and Lorna Touryan Miller, and Jenny Wannier, putting up with my multiple requests while editing.

I also want to thank the other members of my family, specially my daughters Ani, Tamara and Lena and my grandchildren Beatrice, Noah and Lydia for their continued interest, suggestions and support of my work.

Last but not least I need to recognize the invaluable service and support of my wife Alice who, while working on her own family memoirs, would constantly remind me to work on mine instead of getting side-tracked by other projects. We had spent innumerable hours while travelling in the car as she was reading my manuscript and tried to correct sentence structure, syntax and proper usage and phrasing. Without her persistent energy, drive, good cooking and support this work could not have been completed.

Otherwise any errors and omissions that are present in the manuscript are solely mine and I would like to be informed of it.

Send your emails, hopefully positive comments and constructive criticism to gketabgian@yahoo.com.

www.ingramcontent.com/pod-product-compliance
Lightning Source LLC
Chambersburg PA
CBHW051043160426
43193CB00010B/1049